FIGHTING
for the
FOREST

Also by P. O'Connell Pearson

Fly Girls

FIGHTING

for the

FOREST

How FDR's Civilian Conservation Corps Helped Save America

P. O'Connell Pearson

Simon & Schuster Books for Young Readers

NEW YORK   LONDON   TORONTO   SYDNEY   NEW DELHI

SIMON & SCHUSTER BOOKS FOR YOUNG READERS

An imprint of Simon & Schuster Children's Publishing Division

1230 Avenue of the Americas, New York, New York 10020

SIMON & SCHUSTER BOOKS FOR YOUNG READERS

is a trademark of Simon & Schuster, Inc.

For information about special discounts for bulk purchases, please contact Simon & Schuster Special Sales at 1-866-506-1949 or business@simonandschuster.com.

The Simon & Schuster Speakers Bureau can bring authors to your live event. For more information or to book an event, contact the Simon & Schuster Speakers Bureau at 1-866-248-3049 or visit our website at www.simonspeakers.com.

Also available in a Simon & Schuster Books for Young Readers hardcover edition

Cover design by Greg Stadnyk

Interior design by Hilary Zarycky

The text for this book was set in New Caledonia LT Std.

Manufactured in the United States of America 0820 MTN

First Simon & Schuster Books for Young Readers paperback edition October 2020

2 4 6 8 10 9 7 5 3

Library of Congress Control Number 2019946435

ISBN 978-1-5344-2932-1 (hc)

ISBN 978-1-5344-2933-8 (pbk)

ISBN 978-1-5344-2934-5 (eBook)

For Paul

ACKNOWLEDGMENTS

My fondness for the Civilian Conservation Corps goes back to my earliest visits to Shenandoah National Park in Virginia many years ago. Doing the research for this book reinforced my affection for the young men who served in the CCC and increased my admiration for the program and the people responsible for it. I appreciate all those who are working today to preserve the Civilian Conservation Corps' legacy, including the National Association Civilian Conservation Corps Alumni, the Civilian Conservation Corps Legacy, and the Living New Deal, as well as the men and women who work for the National Park Service, the United States Forest Service, and the various state park and forest systems.

A heartfelt thanks to my dear friend Doris Wilson Rosenberg, who so generously shared her father Woody's stories, pictures, and documents; and to mentor and friend Susan E. Goodman, who saw me through the first draft of the book at Lesley University with expertise and enthusiasm. Thanks also to my editor at Simon & Schuster, Liz Kossnar, for her encouragement and keen eye; copy editor, Valerie Shea, for an outstanding job; and Greg Stadnyk, for a cover that captures the CCC perfectly. I am also indebted to Chief Historian for the US Forest Service Lincoln Bramwell, PhD, who readily shared his time and knowledge.

Finally, I am forever grateful to the friends and family who allow me to go on and on with every new thing I learn in the research process and who are always willing to ask me how the writing is going. My gratitude and love especially to my children and grandchildren and to my husband, Paul, whose support is endless.

CONTENTS

FDR (right) and Herbert Hoover (left) en route to the US Capitol for Roosevelt's inauguration in 1933.

CHAPTER 1

Waiting for Hope

In the gray, cold morning of March 4, 1933, Franklin Delano Roosevelt woke in his room at the Mayflower Hotel in Washington, DC. This was a big day, perhaps the biggest day of Roosevelt's life. But he started the morning the same way he had for years at home in New York—he ate breakfast in bed. Roosevelt wasn't lazy, not a bit. As governor of New York, he had often worked while he ate—reading newspapers and going over important documents. Then a personal aide would take away the breakfast tray and lift Roosevelt from the bed to a wheelchair and help him use the bathroom. FDR was used to this morning routine, used to having someone help him with the most basic things. His legs had been completely paralyzed for nearly twelve years.

Once the aide helped him into his underthings, Roosevelt strapped on the metal braces that allowed him to stand up for short periods of time. Though the braces were heavy and uncomfortable, they were frequently part of FDR's routine. On most days, Roosevelt wore a business suit. But on this morning, he chose formal striped trousers and a morning coat. After all, at noon Franklin Delano Roosevelt would be inaugurated president of the United States.

Meanwhile, in Herndon, Virginia, twenty-five miles west of Washington, Woody Wilson started his own morning routine. It was nothing like Mr. Roosevelt's. The walk from Woody's back door to the outhouse could be frigid on such a damp day, but he was used to it, never having had an indoor toilet. He was also used to wearing the same worn clothes day after day, because that was all he owned. Eighteen-year-old Walker Woodrow Wilson—named for President Woodrow Wilson, who was in office when he was born—lived with his parents in the small house his father had built. He would have liked to be out on his own like his five older brothers and sisters were, but he didn't see a way to do it. Woody was stuck with no money, no job, and no place to find work. He'd quit school five years earlier at the end of eighth grade and found temporary jobs here and there for a while. But for the last three years—well, the economy had been in ruins. Woody couldn't even find enough work to help his parents buy food for the three of them, and it hurt to feel useless, especially with his father unemployed.

Thomas Wilson, Woody's dad, had worked for years on the railroad that collected milk from dairy farms in Virginia's hilly countryside and delivered it to the dairies that processed it in and near Washington, DC. Back and forth, every day—hundreds of gallons of milk. But people could no longer afford to buy all that milk or any of the other factory and farm goods that trains hauled.[1] As a result, Tom Wilson lost his job. And he wasn't alone.

All over the United States, thousands and thousands of men and women faced unemployment as the big spending of the 1920s slowed and the economy slid into a depression: a depression that had worsened every day for three years. How had it happened?

Economic depressions are like the flu: contagious. Suppose a factory closes and the workers lose their jobs. Since they don't have money coming in, they stop buying new clothes. After a while the clothing stores go out of business and those workers lose *their* jobs. The factory workers and the clothing store workers stop going to restaurants. Pretty soon the restaurants close and *those* workers lose *their* jobs. The spiral widens and widens, pulling everything down with it, like water swirling into a drain.

There had been depressions before, but none like the one that started in 1929 and became known as the Great Depression ("great" meaning huge, not wonderful). The stock market—where people can buy small pieces, or shares, of businesses in hopes of making a profit when they sell their shares later—had crashed. Instead of growing, businesses failed and the shares many people had spent their savings on were now worthless. Banks collapsed and lost their customers' savings. Thousands of factories went bankrupt, leaving their workers without jobs. As everything fell apart, people wanted to know why it had all happened. But

Economies and Depressions

An *economy* is everything anyone in a country does to make, buy, and sell goods and services. That includes finding resources, building factories, hiring workers, trucking goods to stores, advertising, and on and on. When the economy is doing well, most people can find jobs and afford decent housing and food. An economy that is doing *very* well is said to be in a boom. When economic activity slows down, people lose jobs, buy fewer things, and spend less money. That means that they can't afford the things they normally buy, and businesses can't sell everything they produce. An economic slowdown is called a *recession*. A very serious slowdown is called a *depression*. The worldwide depression that started in 1929 was the worst economic slowdown in modern history. It lasted for a decade and is known as the Great Depression.

three years later, on Franklin Roosevelt's Inauguration Day, ordinary people like the Wilsons didn't care anymore about what had caused the Great Depression. They didn't care why the stock market had collapsed or why banks lost all that money. They just wanted to know what the new president was going to do to fix things so they could find jobs again and be able to feed, clothe, and house their families.

At ten fifteen, President-Elect Roosevelt, his wife, Eleanor, and their invited guests entered St. John's Episcopal Church near the White House for a brief service. Some members of the congregation saw that Mr. Roosevelt kept his head bowed for a very long time. Thinking about the economic crisis and the problems FDR would face as president, they decided that if he was praying for strength and guidance, he had good reason. Meanwhile, a mile east at the end of the National Mall, reporters and cameramen tried to ignore the bone-chilling wind as they set up their equipment on the grounds of the United States Capitol. The streets in Washington had been nearly empty earlier in the morning, but now people began to gather. Hundreds and then thousands of spectators made their way toward the lawn in front of the huge domed building. They stamped their feet and pulled their scarves tighter against the cold as they waited for the ceremony to begin—but they didn't say much to one another. One man said the crowd was "as silent as a group of mourners around a grave."[2]

• • •

The mood was the same around the rest of the country. On most Saturday mornings people would be busy with trips to the market, the barbershop, the bank, and more. But during the past week, the governors of most states had ordered all the banks to close. So many banks had failed—and so many others teetered on the edge of failing—that the governors feared violence and rioting. That had already happened in some places when banks couldn't give customers the money that was supposed to be in their accounts. People had panicked.

With all the banks closed, even men and women who had money in a solid, safe bank couldn't get to it. Businesses couldn't pay their workers. Guests at fine hotels in Washington who'd come for the inauguration couldn't cover the cost of their rooms. This was long before credit cards or ATMs, so what were people supposed to do?

Just before eleven o'clock, Roosevelt arrived at the north entrance to the White House in the back of an open touring car, a convertible. He waited with a heavy blanket over his thin, braced legs as President Herbert Hoover came to join him. The two men rode toward the Capitol together, hardly speaking at all. There really wasn't anything to say. Hoover had run for a second term against Roosevelt in November and been trounced. He knew Americans were angry as well as frightened. During the presidential campaign, some people had even thrown rotten eggs at his car as he rode by.[3] Four years earlier, Herbert Hoover had won election easily. But now voters blamed him for the terrible financial disaster that was destroying their lives and their country. The blame wasn't entirely fair.

The Depression began about eight months after Hoover took office in 1929. But the problems that led to it had been growing for several years. When the economy fell, Hoover actually did more to try to lift businesses and banks than any president had ever done before. However, nothing he did seemed to help, and millions of Americans found themselves hungry and homeless.

For three years President Hoover assured Americans that the economy was getting better even when everyone knew it was getting worse. He tried to explain that he was doing everything a president *could* do, and he meant what he said. He believed that "voluntary organizations and community service"—people helping one another—were the best way to get money and food to the needy. The federal government (the government of the whole country) didn't belong in citizens' personal economic lives.[4] But the crisis was too deep. As Inauguration Day approached, Hoover told an aide, "We are at the end of our string. There is nothing more we can do."[5]

Franklin Roosevelt disagreed. He believed that in such terrible circumstances the federal government *had* to save people from starvation and save the country from collapse. Roosevelt was convinced that there was much, much more the government and the president could do to turn things around.

When Election Day came in November 1932, voters rejected Hoover's philosophy and elected Franklin Roosevelt in a landslide.

What Caused the Great Depression?

Several factors came together to cause the Great Depression. During the 1920s, many businesses used their profits to buy new equipment and build new factories but didn't increase workers' pay. As a result, workers couldn't afford to buy things, which left business owners with warehouses full of goods they couldn't sell. They slowed their production and had to fire workers. At the same time, demand for farm goods, which had increased during World War I, now fell. Farmers couldn't make enough money to pay back the money they had borrowed to buy new tractors and the like. Additionally, many banks used the money their customers had put in savings accounts to invest in risky businesses. When those businesses failed, the banks could not give customers their money. That, in turn, caused panic at other banks. Problems in international trade also hurt the economy. The result was a severe, worldwide depression.

Roosevelt waved his hat to the crowds that now filled sidewalks and stretched over the stairs and porches of office buildings on Pennsylvania Avenue. People cheered when they saw the president-elect's jaunty smile. They hoped that smile meant help was on the way and everything would be all right. They hoped the country had made the right choice.

FDR looked confident and energetic. He knew it was important for people to see that their president believed the situation would improve. But even as he lifted his top hat to his supporters, he was well aware of the grim statistics he and the nation faced. He knew the numbers that kept economic experts awake at night. Those numbers told a terrible story.

Let's start with the number twenty-five. Twenty-five percent of the workers in the United States were unemployed in 1933. The US had never had such high unemployment before and never has since. Not even close.

Like Woody's family in Virginia, most families in those days relied on just one worker to provide all the money for housing, clothing, and food. If that one worker lost his job, it left the whole family with no income—so when one hundred people lost their jobs, four or five hundred people found themselves in need. Twenty-five percent unemployment meant that millions of American workers and their families had absolutely no income. In addition, millions more men and women had gone from full-time to part-time employment, some working as little as one day a week. Even people who still had their regular jobs often had a hard time because they had to support their own families *and* out-of-work brothers, sisters, parents, or other relatives.

To make matters worse, the government provided no "safety net" programs at the time—programs to help people who can't find jobs. No unemployment insurance, and no government help with the cost of food, housing, medical needs, or anything else. If a jobless person couldn't get aid from extended family and local charities that had nothing left to give, that person had nowhere to turn.

Across the country, millions of Americans lived on cheap oatmeal and macaroni meal after meal. They gave up their telephones and turned off the heat. Sometimes they turned off the electricity as well. They brushed with baking soda instead of toothpaste, put cardboard in their shoes to cover the holes, and even used the pages of free shopping catalogs in place of toilet paper. "Use it up, wear it out, make it do, or do without" became their motto. Even so, starvation was a real possibility.

Numbers such as unemployment percentages are averages, of course. While unemployment wasn't nearly as high as 25 percent in some places, it was much higher in others. In Detroit, Michigan, for example, a young man named Houston Pritchett had worked hard to finish high school, beating the odds for African American men in the 1930s. Only one-third of all young Americans had high school diplomas in those days, and the rate for blacks was far less than that. But even with a diploma, Houston couldn't find a job. Unemployment in Detroit was 50 percent overall and much worse for African Americans, and Houston Pritchett spent his days in the streets, terribly poor.[6] Thousands of other young men like him did the same. They stood on corners or huddled in doorways, and when their hunger got too bad, they sometimes turned to stealing food, or money to get food.

In Toledo, Ohio, the situation was unbelievably awful. Unemployment there neared 80 percent.[7] Think about that. Eight out of ten workers in Toledo had no jobs. That meant that eight out of ten families, or at least 230,000 of the 290,000 men, women, and children in the city had no income.[8] What could the new president promise people in Detroit and Toledo? What could he do to help people like Woody Wilson and Houston Pritchett and their families?

While President-elect Roosevelt and President Hoover rode slowly toward the Capitol, the people Roosevelt had invited to the prayer service struggled to get from the church to the inaugural ceremony. Cabinet members and many other guests were expected to sit behind the new president as he took the oath of office and gave his inaugural address. But there had never been so many people in Washington, and the huge crowds made getting to the Capitol difficult. Men and women packed the sidewalks and hundreds of pedestrians blocked traffic as they spilled into the street.

Frances Perkins, about to become the first woman ever appointed to a presidential cabinet, tried to find a taxi outside St. John's Church. She had no luck. Neither did Henry Wallace, soon to be secretary of agriculture. Together, they flagged down an ordinary car and begged the driver to help. He took them as far as he could, but the crowd was too thick. Anxious to be on time for the ceremony, Perkins and Wallace jumped out of the car and ran up Pennsylvania Avenue, pushing their way through the crowd. They ducked under a police rope and onto the cold, wet lawn, where Frances Perkins's high heels sank into the soggy grass. They raced up the Capitol's steps and, gasping for air, slipped into their seats as the inauguration got underway. They had nearly missed the first official duty of the first day in their new jobs.[9]

Both Perkins and Wallace were newcomers to Washington, and both were anxious to get busy. They knew how desperate the country was.

Frances Perkins had worked with terribly poor people in huge cities like Chicago and New York. She'd fought for better conditions for men and women in dangerous factory jobs, where workers often lost fingers or hands in machinery or inhaled fabric fibers or coal dust day in and day out. As bad as those jobs were, though, they were better than no job at all. And many of those people were now out of work. Perkins knew the workers' children, who went to school ashamed of being constantly dirty and smelly since they had no hot water for a bath. Many stayed home from school in bitter cold weather because they owned no coats, mittens, or boots. Instead of learning anything or playing outside or seeing other children, they stayed in bed and under blankets and quilts in their unheated homes.

Millions of children also suffered from malnutrition because they didn't have enough to eat and rarely got fruits or vegetables or good protein.[10] In Woody's home state of Virginia, 90 percent of the children in schools were malnourished.[11] And when a teacher in Washington, DC, asked a boy why he hadn't brought lunch to school, he answered, "It's my sister's turn to eat today."[12] Lack of good food left children too weak to fight off colds or other illnesses. Their noses ran constantly, they had no energy, and their skin turned scaly and dry. Poor nutrition could also lead to diseases such as scurvy, which causes exhaustion and pain, and rickets, which softens a child's bones.

Imagine going whole days with nothing to eat or putting ketchup on a piece of bread and calling it dinner. Children felt real pain in their stomachs because of the hunger. They went to bed hungry and woke to go to school without breakfast. Picture feeling that way day after day and knowing each night that the next day would be no better. In the years before school lunch programs for the poor, thousands of teachers used their own money to buy food for their students, but other teachers couldn't do that—many of them were just as poor as the children they taught. Misery spread everywhere.

The Depression had forced entire families to live in their cars or trucks, or cram into cardboard and scrap-wood shacks in camps called "Hoovervilles." These shantytowns appeared on the edges of nearly every city and town in the country, often close to rivers, where people could use river water to wash, no matter how dirty it might be. Five-year-olds begged on the streets of places like St. Louis and Baltimore. And men who had been previously well-off stood on corners selling apples or wearing signs asking for food.

Churches, synagogues, and charities turned their basements and hallways into makeshift kitchens where a person could get a free meal. Hungry people stood in "bread lines" that stretched out the door and around the block. Houston Pritchett waited in a line like that almost every day for a bowl of thin soup and a little bread. Often, it was all he had to eat. Thousands more hungry men and women prowled alleys behind restaurants and markets, foraging for food in garbage bins, their mouths and noses covered with handkerchiefs to mask the stench of rotting meat.

Eighty years later, one woman, her voice breaking with emotion, said, "You can't imagine how poor people were. You can't imagine it."[13]

The misery hit big cities, small towns like Herndon, and even the farmlands of America. Henry Wallace, Roosevelt's choice for secretary of agriculture, came from Iowa and knew more about farming than almost anyone. He understood the hardships agricultural families experienced. Just like city homeowners, farmers borrowed money to build barns or houses or buy land and equipment. But when farm incomes dropped, they couldn't pay the banks what they owed and the banks could take their land in what's called *foreclosure*. By Inauguration Day, nearly one-third of the farmers on the Great Plains—the dry grasslands that stretch east to west between the Missouri River and the Rocky Mountains—faced foreclosure on their land. The same was true of ranchers in Texas, Oklahoma, Colorado, and elsewhere.[14]

Farmers in every part of the country who'd been doing well a decade ago were now bankrupt. The land simply wasn't producing what it used to, or prices for crops had fallen to practically nothing, or both. Farm children suffered red, itchy skin when their mothers were forced to dress them in shirts or smocks made of old feed sacks. And most went without shoes much of the year. How would the nation survive if something wasn't done?

Throughout the United States, workers with and without jobs, families in marble mansions and in tar-paper shacks, farmers watching spring rains irrigate their fields and farmers seeing the dry soil turn to dust—all gathered around the nearest radio on Inauguration Day. They wanted to hear the new president speak. Americans everywhere—those who had voted for Roosevelt and those who had not—sensed change was coming. Most hoped that it was.

Millions had nothing left but hope.

Outside the US Capitol during FDR's inauguration in 1933.

CHAPTER 2

Taking Action

Under the United States Constitution, Americans elect a president every four years. George Washington was the first man elected, of course, and Franklin Roosevelt was the thirty-second. Whoever is elected officially becomes president only after taking the presidential oath of office. That is the only requirement found in the Constitution, but starting with George Washington, incoming presidents take that oath at a very formal inauguration ceremony like Roosevelt's. (When a president dies in office, the vice president takes the oath and becomes president as quickly as possible without any ceremony.)

Over the years, a number of traditions have developed around the inauguration. Roosevelt followed one of those traditions when he rode to the Capitol with the outgoing president. The simple ride down Pennsylvania Avenue has become a symbol that in the United States, leaders give up their power peacefully when a new leader is elected and that the two are not enemies. Another tradition started when George Washington put one hand on a Bible as he took the presidential oath of office. The Constitution makes clear that "no religious test shall ever be required as a qualification to an office" in the United States. But a majority of presidents since Washington have followed his example in using a Bible, and Roosevelt planned to use his family's two-hundred-year-old Dutch Bible. (Some presidents have used books of law, and FDR's cousin Theodore did not use a book of any kind.)

Franklin Roosevelt also planned to give his inaugural speech from the East Front of the Capitol, a tradition begun by Andrew Jackson in 1833 (lasting until 1981; presidents are now inaugurated on the West Front of the Capitol, facing the National Mall and Lincoln Memorial). And like many other presidents, he chose formal clothing to demonstrate his respect for the event and the presidency. But there was one tradition Franklin Roosevelt could not keep. Since Andrew Jackson's time, incoming presidents had climbed the East Front's graceful marble stairs to reach the Capitol's Rotunda—the big, circular room under the Capitol's dome. Roosevelt's heavy leg braces helped him stand because they kept his knees from bending when they were locked in place. But neither the braces nor anything else would allow him to climb a single step. No one with paralyzed legs could get up the Capitol's beautiful staircase.

Carpenters had built a series of ramps so FDR could be wheeled up to the Rotunda. They covered the ramps with maroon carpet and enclosed them with wooden walls and a roof to keep them dry. The walls also gave Mr. Roosevelt the privacy he wanted. He enjoyed being out among the American people, but he hated having anyone who didn't know him well see him be lifted into and out of a wheelchair like a rag doll—he knew most people were uncomfortable with someone in a wheelchair. They didn't know where to look, he claimed, or what to say.[15] FDR hid his disability whenever he could.

As inauguration time approached, the swelling crowd on the Capitol grounds formed a sea of dark overcoats and felt hats pulled low against the wind. Reporters spoke into radio micro-phones to describe the quiet crowd, the damp, cold day, and the guests gathering on the stage. Layers of thick garlands decorated the Capitol's marble railings, and more draped the high portico ceiling. Huge flags hung behind the building's imposing columns.

Cameramen filmed members of Congress, the new cabinet officers, and the Roosevelt family as they arrived. Their canisters of film would be rushed by train and small planes to hundreds of theaters around the country later in the day.

At exactly one o'clock, Franklin Roosevelt came through the massive bronze doors of the Capitol. He was holding the arm of his son James, who would bear a lot of his weight when he made his way down a ramp and across the platform. The Marine Corps Band struck up "Hail to the Chief." Roosevelt held his chin high and his back straight and, still holding his son's arm, started mov-ing stiff-legged toward the podium.

This moment was more than a political triumph for FDR. It was a much more personal triumph as well.

There was no doubt that Franklin Delano Roosevelt was coming to the presidency well-prepared. He'd grown up admiring and sometimes imitating President Theodore Roosevelt, his fifth cousin—meaning they shared a great-great-great-great-grandfather who'd come to America in the 1600s (Theodore was also the uncle of FDR's wife Eleanor, making Franklin and Eleanor fifth cousins once removed). He'd attended Harvard University and Columbia Law School and appreciated the power and importance of the law. He had gained political experience as a New York state senator and later as the 1920 Democratic candidate for vice president with James Cox (they lost). FDR had also learned how the federal government and the military worked through his time as assistant secretary of the navy during World War I. People thought of the young Franklin Roosevelt as smart, likable, energetic, and good-looking, and by 1921, at the age of thirty-nine, he had enough experience and support to be a good candidate for the House of Representatives or the United States Senate or governor of New York.

However, everything changed overnight that summer of 1921. After a day of boating and swimming with his family, Roosevelt felt unusually tired and went to bed early. When he awoke the next morning, he was feverish and his legs were too weak to hold him. FDR had contracted polio. For weeks, he suffered from a high fever and pain, but eventually recovered and regained complete movement in his upper body. However, though he fought with determination and grit, he couldn't undo what the disease had done to his legs. He remained paralyzed from the waist down.

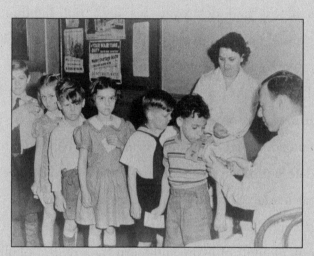

What Is Polio?

Polio, or poliomyelitis, was a frightening disease in the 1920s and thirties. The virus most often attacked children and usually caused flu-like symptoms. But some victims experienced more serious effects, including paralysis. If the paralysis affected the throat or chest, it could be deadly. When it attacked arms or legs, it left people disabled for life (FDR was paralyzed from the waist down). There is still no cure for polio, but Dr. Jonas Salk developed the first polio vaccine to prevent the disease in the 1950s. The vaccine gave a person a weak bit of the disease that caused the body to build its immune system against that particular germ. Today, the vaccine is made from a killed germ. Since Salk's breakthrough, vaccinations have nearly eliminated polio in most of the world.

Most people he knew, even his mother, told him his paralysis meant the end of his political career, the shattering of his dreams. They were sure that Americans would never vote for a man in a wheelchair.

Roosevelt's wife, Eleanor, and a few close friends disagreed. FDR's illness had destroyed his legs, but fighting to regain strength had taught him self-discipline. Learning to live without being able to stand or walk had given him patience. He'd also gained new respect for how hard life could be and learned to sympathize with ordinary people whose troubles he had never experienced. Eleanor believed Franklin had had a lot to offer as a candidate before his illness, but now, he would be an even better political leader. She later said, "Franklin's illness . . . gave him strength and courage he had not had before. He had to think out the fundamentals of living and learn the greatest of all lessons— infinite patience and never ending persistence."[16]

Franklin Roosevelt returned to politics and campaigning. But the fact remained that many Americans assumed anyone in a wheelchair was too weak to hold an important and difficult position in government. So before he ran for office again, FDR devised a way to stand and "walk" for very short distances. With ten pounds of metal bracing him, his legs couldn't buckle, and he learned to throw one hip forward and then the other. This motion swung his withered legs ahead. He exercised every day to keep his upper body strong enough to manage the movement, but the physical effort and the pain of the braces were exhausting.

It didn't matter. Roosevelt was determined to *look* like he was walking and smile while he did it. His act worked.

Roosevelt wasn't dishonest about his polio. People everywhere knew he'd been stricken, and it was obvious that he couldn't walk without help. But his ability to stand tall and straight let the public look past what he *couldn't* do and focus on what he *could* do. Americans saw a wealthy man with an upper-class accent, a lot of government and political experience, and a winning smile who somehow understood their problems. They saw a man who had had polio but who had overcome it. And though FDR hadn't completely overcome polio physically, he had beaten it in ways that mattered even more. He hadn't let it steal his dreams or his optimism. He hadn't let it destroy his plans for the future. Roosevelt was elected governor of New York in 1928 and again in 1930, gaining additional political experience. When he ran for president in 1932, voters recognized not only his political preparation, they also recognized him as a man who knew how to overcome obstacles. No economic disaster was going to defeat anyone with such "bottomless reserves of physical and mental strength."[17]

Solemnly, Franklin Delano Roosevelt swore to "preserve, protect, and defend the Constitution of the United States." Then he turned to face the audience.

Roosevelt knew democracy was at risk. People in some European countries had even turned to dictators who promised better times. But was that the kind of government Americans wanted?

Roosevelt thought not. Yet he realized how important his inaugural address was. If he was going to succeed as president in such a terrible situation, he had to have the nation's support. He needed to be honest and realistic about the crisis, but at the same time, he had to give people hope.

In most campaign speeches, FDR had impressed people with his cheerful, buoyant way of talking. His smile seemed to come right through the radio waves. Now as he stood at the microphone in the cold March wind, his voice carried no smile. It was "time to speak the truth, the whole truth, frankly and boldly," he told the country.[18]

Though Roosevelt looked and sounded as serious as Americans felt, he spoke confidently, saying, "Let me assert my firm belief that the only thing we have to fear is fear itself—nameless, unreasoning, unjustified terror which paralyzes needed efforts to convert retreat into advance."[19]

The president admitted that the economy couldn't be fixed easily or quickly. But he reminded people of the country's great resources and potential. If everyone pulled together, he said, they could defeat the Great Depression. Bursts of polite applause gave way to genuine enthusiasm as he went on. FDR sounded certain that the United States would survive, certain that Americans would overcome the enormous obstacles they faced.

This nation asks for action, and action now. Our
greatest primary task is to put people to work. This

is no unsolvable problem if we face it wisely and
courageously. . . . There are many ways in which it
can be helped, but it can never be helped merely
by talking about it. We must act and act quickly.[20]

In Washington, the crowd cheered, and some waved hand-kerchiefs. Frances Perkins described seeing "tears streaming down the faces of strong men"[21] as the new president spoke, and another woman said, "Any man who can talk like that in times like these is worthy of every ounce of support a true American has."[22]

When the ceremony ended, FDR and his family had a simple lunch and then watched the inaugural parade from a viewing stand on Pennsylvania Avenue—another tradition. Eighteen thousand marchers in bands and military units made their way down the wide street while a crowd ten deep filled the stands, sidewalks, rooftops, and trees along the route. Roosevelt appeared to be delighted with the festivities, despite the weather. But he was anxious to get to work—he had promised action. "More power to you, Mr. Roosevelt," one reporter said for a newsreel. "The entire country is behind you, filled with hope and patriotism."[23]

The Roosevelts had dinner with a large group of friends and family before First Lady Eleanor Roosevelt left the White House and rode to the traditional inaugural ball wearing a slate-blue silk gown. She and other family members greeted her husband's supporters graciously, but the president himself was nowhere to be seen. As much as he liked tradition, Roosevelt had decided not to attend this event.

FDR enjoyed balls as a young man. He had first invited Eleanor to dance with him at a Christmas party when he was sixteen and she was fourteen.[24] Now though, it pained him to watch everyone else on the dance floor while he sat in a chair. But there was much more to his absence than that. He knew that this was no time for the president to attend parties.

Lights burned in government offices that night as Roosevelt talked with his advisers and his aides worked on the plans he wanted for every part of the economy. During the next few days and nights, FDR held meeting after meeting to discuss ideas for attacking the Great Depression.

Just five days after taking office, on March 9, Roosevelt brought his cabinet—the heads of all the major government departments—together to talk about the programs he intended to propose to Congress. Together, those programs became known as the New Deal. Roosevelt was ready to try all kinds of ideas. As he said, "It is common sense to take a method and try it. If it fails, admit it frankly and try another. But above all, try something."[25] He and his advisers had come up with lots of somethings, and his enthusiasm for the proposals he had settled on was obvious to everyone.

FDR intended to ask Congress for laws to protect the money people put in banks to give them confidence in those banks and avoid panics in the future. He had a plan for bringing electricity

MORE SECURITY FOR THE AMERICAN FAMILY

THE WIDOW OF A QUALIFIED WORKER WILL RECEIVE MONTHLY BENEFITS AT AGE 65. IN CERTAIN CASES, AN AGED DEPENDENT PARENT MAY GET BENEFITS. ...

FOR INFORMATION WRITE OR CALL AT THE NEAREST FIELD OFFICE OF THE
SOCIAL SECURITY BOARD

The New Deal

In July 1932, Franklin Roosevelt won the Democratic nomination for president. He gave a memorable speech when he accepted the nomination, and near the end, he said, "I pledge you, I pledge myself, to a new deal for the American people."[149] Reporters quoted that phrase, and by the time Roosevelt became president, his plans to confront the Great Depression were known as the New Deal. The New Deal included programs to give people jobs, to get the economy working again, and to prevent future depressions. Sometimes called alphabet soup, programs such as the Civilian Conservation Corps went by their initials—the CCC, WPA (Works Progress Administration), TVA (Tennessee Valley Authority), and so on. Most were temporary programs, but some—Social Security, the Soil Conservation Service (now the Natural Resource Conservation Service), and others—still exist today.

to the poorest rural areas in the country to improve businesses and lives. He also wanted to hire construction workers to build monuments and government buildings, including a new home for the Supreme Court, and improvements to the Washington Monument and Lincoln Memorial. Similar projects could be done nationwide. But one program stood out from the others as being very near to Roosevelt's heart. It was an idea he had promoted for years.

Franklin Roosevelt planned to recruit five hundred thousand young men and put them to work on conservation projects around the country. He saw the plan as "killing two birds with one stone . . . conserving not only our natural resources, but our human resources."[26]

A few cabinet secretaries nodded and smiled at the president's idea for a civilian conservation corps, as he called it. But none of them—not the secretary of labor, secretary of the interior, secretary of agriculture, or any of the others—imagined such a project would be simple. In some ways it sounded absurd. Did the president really want to solve environmental problems using a half-million poor city boys who had never been in the country? Were they what he meant by human resources?

Woody Wilson would never have called himself a human resource. Neither would Houston Pritchett or other young men like them. But their president did. He knew that leaving young men like Woody and Houston on street corners in Herndon or bread lines in Detroit was bad for them and for the country. Roosevelt said later,

No country, however rich, can afford the waste of its human resources. Demoralization caused by vast unemployment is our greatest extravagance. Morally, it is the greatest menace to our social order.[27]

FDR realized that losing a job took away more than a person's income. It took away that person's dignity and feeling of worth, of being useful. Vast unemployment led to crime and tore families apart. Men, in particular, lost confidence and self-esteem without jobs.

Most people growing up in the United States in the early twentieth century believed that men and women had very clear responsibilities in life. A man was supposed to work hard and provide for his family. He was supposed to keep his wife and children safe and secure. Men generally didn't do housework or take care of children—that was the woman's responsibility. So a man without a job was not fulfilling his purpose and was a failure, not a real man.

That was why men like Tom Wilson, Woody's dad, had such a hard time asking for help from grown children or elderly parents. It was why young men like Woody Wilson and Houston Pritchett felt useless. They couldn't see a future for themselves. They couldn't look forward to their adult lives because they couldn't do the things that would define them as grown up.

Roosevelt understood that those young men needed jobs if

they were ever going to feel like good, productive citizens. He knew there were a lot of ways to put people to work on useful projects, and he wanted to explore every possibility. But FDR was certain that his conservation corps was the best way to help young men. Similar but smaller programs had been tried in Europe and in several states, and as governor of New York, Roosevelt had put poor young men to work in state parks and forests. He had no doubt that clean air, decent food, and hard physical work could do great things for a young man's health and confidence. In his inaugural address, Roosevelt had talked about "greatly needed projects to stimulate and reorganize the use of our great natural resources." That was what he had in mind for the conservation corps.

Some advisers wondered if this was really the time to spend federal tax money on conserving natural resources. As good as it sounded to give the unemployed jobs in the great outdoors, could the country really afford such projects in the midst of the nation's worst-ever economic crisis?

Franklin Roosevelt argued that the country *had* to afford such projects. The nation's economy depended on its natural resources, and those resources were in trouble. Agriculture, for example, had always been a big part of America's economic success. Farms produced the food people around the country ate. In fact, American farms produced enough food to keep prices fairly low. Farms also produced food products for export to other countries. But if the nation lost huge amounts of its farmland to drought or declining soil, the cost of food and other products would go up, and workers in the factories that made cereals and bread or canned vegetables and fruits and the like would lose their jobs.

Forestry was another issue. The millions of acres of huge, ancient trees in America had once seemed endless, but by 1900 forest experts believed that America's forests would soon be so overused that they could not produce enough wood for building houses, fences, and furniture, and making paper and other products. Shortages would push prices up and would also mean the loss of jobs in construction, and at factories and mills. The effects would spill into every part of the country. This was one reason for the push to create national forests and the effort had saved millions of acres of trees. A timber shortage was no longer likely, but those forests had been neglected in recent years and faced new dangers.

And parks. Well, parks played a different kind of role. It was easy to say that the government couldn't afford to spend money on picnic areas, public gardens, and other frivolous-sounding outdoor spaces. But the fact was that parks are worthwhile investments. Parks' trees help keep the air and water clean and provide refuge for wildlife. They also offer people opportunities to interact with nature and improve their physical and mental health. Before 1920, the majority of Americans lived in rural areas. By the 1930s, though, more than half the people in the United States lived in cities and towns, and public parks and forests became more important than ever. Building parks would provide jobs to the men of the conservation corps and also to people who sold tools and work boots and all the other things the men would need. The same was true of restoring forests and farmland.

"Men and nature must work hand in hand," Roosevelt said. It was the responsibility of the federal government to rescue and

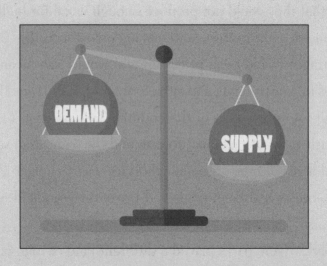

Supply and Demand

Suppose there is only one pizza restaurant in town, and that restaurant can make fifty pizzas each day. The fifty pizzas are called supply. People who want to buy pizza create demand. If there are fifty pizzas and eighty people who each want to buy one, demand is greater than supply. The restaurant can now charge more for its pizza since at least fifty of those eighty people may be willing to pay more to get what they want. If only thirty people want pizza, the restaurant might lower its price in order to encourage more people to buy. The law of supply and demand says that when supply is low and demand is high, prices go up, and when supply is high and demand is low, prices go down.

protect the environment and be sure resources were used wisely. Some people disagreed on the role of government in protecting or restoring the environment (and people still disagree today). But FDR had studied history and was confident that he was following in the footsteps of our greatest presidents.

Mammoth Hot Springs at Yellowstone National Park in 1872.

CHAPTER 3

Looking Back

A mericans have had a complicated relationship with nature and natural resources since the first Englishmen arrived in North America in the 1600s. The newcomers settled along the eastern coastline, where they found thick forests, clear, clean rivers and springs, and more fish and game than they had ever imagined. Europe had almost no wilderness or unused land at the time, and the natural wealth in America felt endless.

Additionally, eastern North America was much less densely populated than the European continent most settlers had left. Even so, the Europeans soon pushed those native peoples who were there out of their region. With seemingly infinite land, the early European Americans didn't often think about protecting or conserving resources the way native peoples did.

By the time the original thirteen colonies declared independence from Great Britain in 1776, tobacco had worn out the soil in some places. Fish and game weren't as plentiful as they had been a century earlier either, and the trees weren't as thick. But there was more land just beyond the Appalachian Mountains and even farther west. Why not move there and start again? After the American Revolution, thousands of people pushed across the Appalachians to claim land for new farms and plantations.

George Washington, who had been the leader of the Continental Army during the American Revolution, was a farmer or planter. He owned 7,600 acres of land at his Mount Vernon estate on the Potomac River. Like other plantation owners and small farmers in Virginia, tobacco was his major crop. But Washington found that he couldn't always make a profit with tobacco and saw that years of planting tobacco left the soil almost useless. Rather than abandon his land on the Potomac and start over farther west as some planters did, he began to experiment with other crops.

Washington believed in natural science and used scientific methods to find the best crops for his land (enslaved people did most of the actual labor). He wrote to botanists around the country and in other parts of the world and read everything he could find on the subject. Eventually, he stopped planting large fields of tobacco and made wheat his biggest crop. Then he shared what he had learned with farmers who didn't have enough land or money to experiment on their own. Today, many historians consider Washington the "father of American agriculture."[28]

As the first president of the United States, Washington told Congress in 1790, "There is nothing which can better deserve your patronage [support] than the promotion of science and literature."[29]

He believed the United States could become a leading producer of wheat, corn, and other grains. American farmers could export that grain to countries around the world and bring income to themselves and the nation forever. They could do all that *if* they had the information they needed to make the most of their land.

As the country expanded westward after 1800, American-born and immigrant pioneers settled in river valleys and on forested hills, dry plains, and rain-soaked coastlines. They claimed the free land the government offered and established farms and ranches all the way across the continent. When Abraham Lincoln became president in 1861, over half of all Americans were farmers. Lincoln himself had grown up on frontier farms. As president, he created the Department of Agriculture. Its goal was to educate farmers and ranchers in ways to keep their soil rich and produce the best crops or raise the best livestock possible. The Department would hire scientists to do research and then share their information with farmers and ranchers in every state. Lincoln also signed a law that allowed states to sell federal government land and use the money for schools of agriculture and technology. These "land-grant" colleges—schools such as Cornell, Purdue, MIT, Clemson, and many others— became some of the best research universities in the world.

Of course, land was only one of the abundant resources in the West. Business leaders made fortunes in silver, copper, and gold mining. Others built railroads or went to the western forests to make millions in timber. The opportunities were tremendous, but so were the costs. Ranchers and farmers fenced wild animals out of their natural habitats. Mine owners blasted through mountains, and railroad tycoons hired men to hunt buffalo for food and hides, and to get them out of the way. Timber companies cut whole forests without replanting the landscape, leaving the soil to erode. And tragically, American Indian tribes who had lived on the land for centuries were driven onto reservations and left with nothing. For the next century, presidents continued to ignore Native Americans when they set aside public lands (land that is not owned by a business or individual but by the federal government) and made decisions about how the land would be used. Those policies are still a stain on the United States.

The American wilderness was almost gone by the last half of the nineteenth century, and some people began calling for conservation. Naturalist John Muir worked to protect the western forests, and geologist John Wesley Powell warned of water shortages on farmland and ranchland in the West. They and members of a political movement called Progressivism worried that ancient trees and clean water would soon disappear. Progressives argued that the federal government had to set aside land for parks and national forests before it was too late. In 1872, President Ulysses Grant asked Congress to establish Yellowstone National Park in Wyoming, the first national park in the world.

Thirty years later President Theodore Roosevelt (Franklin Roosevelt's distant cousin) became the first president to make conservation a top priority. TR, a Republican who became president in

1901, had lived in the West as a young man and continued spending as much time as he could outdoors throughout his life. He used his authority as president to protect the land he loved and the animals that lived on it. Most Americans today still think of Theodore Roosevelt when they think of conservation. There's good reason for that.

Before he left office, Teddy Roosevelt set aside over 230 million acres of wild land in the United States—an area nearly the size of Texas and Oklahoma combined. He established or enlarged 150 national forests and put them under the care of the new United States Forest Service. TR created the first national bird reserve (and fifty more after it), four national game preserves, five national parks, and eighteen national monuments. Because of Theodore Roosevelt, places such as the Grand Canyon, Devils Tower, and the Muir Woods were protected from destruction.[30] Most Americans approved of Teddy Roosevelt's actions. But some people, especially those who made money from the country's natural resources, saw TR as an enemy.

Hatmakers (known as milliners) used the feathers of millions of wild birds on the fashionable hats of the time. Timbermen made money by cutting all the trees in huge areas of the national forests, and oil barons drilled on public land wherever and however they could. They and other industrialists, including mine and railroad owners, were furious with the president because he wanted to regulate or limit their private use of public land—land that belonged to the people of the United States. Those business owners believed that public land existed for profit, and that they

Public Lands: Our National Forests and National Parks

National forests and national parks are both public lands, but they are not the same thing. National forests are woodlands and grasslands protected by the United States government. Private businesses such as timber companies and ranchers may take or use these resources with the permission of the USDA Forest Service, which manages them. There are over 150 national forests in the US, made up of nearly 193 million acres of land. Today environmentalists and businesses often argue about the care, use, and management of national forests and grasslands.

A FREE GOVERNMENT SERVICE
GRAND CANYON
NATIONAL PARK
U.S. DEPARTMENT OF THE INTERIOR
NATIONAL PARK SERVICE

The national park system includes fifty-nine parks and a number of other kinds of sites, such as memorials, monuments, parkways, preserves, seashores, and more. Those parks and other sites exist for the education and enjoyment of the public and for future generations. They total over 84 million acres of land nationwide and are managed by the National Park Service. Today conservationists debate how the nation's parks will survive as more and more people visit each year and businesses push to use the parks for profit.

had a right to that profit. Teddy Roosevelt didn't budge, however. He was certain that businesses would do just fine even with regulation. But without regulation, the birds and trees and wilderness would be destroyed. And what then? Where would businesses go for resources? And what about everyone else? TR believed that every American should benefit from the nation's land and water, not just a few business owners.

By the end of his presidency in 1909, Theodore Roosevelt had done more to guard the country's natural resources than any president before him.[31]

The presidents elected during the 1920s generally sided with business on most issues, including the use of public land. They ignored conservationists and allowed industries to mine, drill for oil, and cut trees on that land with almost no supervision at all. Timbermen and oilmen said they would take care of the environment and regulate themselves. They argued that they didn't need government interference. Their promises turned out to be empty and the environmental damage was terrible.

Franklin Roosevelt knew that after so much abuse and neglect, restoring the nation's land would be a gigantic job. But he was more than ready to get started—he'd been studying conservation since he was a child.

The Roosevelt family had lived along the Hudson River in New York for four generations. Franklin's father, James, had inherited a large amount of money and then made even more with his own businesses. Following the family tradition, he bought an estate on the Hudson River near the town of Hyde Park, New York. He named it Springwood, and his son Franklin was born there. Hyde Park, as the family usually called the estate, remained FDR's home for his entire life.

As a boy, Franklin never tired of slogging through winter snow and spring mud, battling mosquitoes in the heat of summer, and kicking through dry fall leaves in the forests on Springwood's six hundred acres. He had a pony and a dog, as well as rabbits and other animals. He learned to swim and sail, went sledding on the estate's hills, and skated on the pond. Most of all, though, he liked to study the birds along the Hudson River and could identify hundreds of species before he was in his teens. As a child, he even sent bird specimens to the American Museum of Natural History in New York City.[32]

Roosevelt's father—who he called Popsy—taught him to recognize the many kinds of trees on the property. In fact, it seemed all the Roosevelt grandparents, aunts, uncles, and cousins loved trees. They planted thousands over the years and worked to keep them healthy. Franklin and his father rode horseback around Springwood, watching the changing seasons and making note of what work needed to be done to maintain their forests. Franklin learned a lot about forestry from his father, and an uncle showed him how to keep soil rich and fertile.[33]

FDR spent nearly all his time at Hyde Park before high school, even working with private tutors instead of going to a regular school. But while a lot of boys would have been terribly bored and lonely without friends their own age, Franklin was always happily busy. Whole days could go by as he climbed trees, watched birds, and went looking for Indian artifacts such as arrowheads.[34]

Young FDR loved to study nature when he went to Europe with his parents, too. He explored community forests in Germany and begged to go to natural history museums in every city they visited.[35] By the time he started high school, Roosevelt knew more about trees, birds, wildlife, and soil than most adults. His interest in nature and conservation continued to grow during his years at Harvard, and later, when he started managing the Roosevelt estate after his father died. The more FDR studied, the more he thought about the way Americans in the twentieth century were using and caring for the nation's vast resources.

World War I (called the Great War at the time) was fought in Europe between 1914 and 1918. Heavy artillery fire destroyed thousands of acres of European farmland, and unexploded shells made farming nearly impossible in many areas. That and food shortages in Great Britain led to a big increase in demand for American wheat, other food crops, and cotton. When the United States entered the war in 1917, demand grew even bigger. Farmers on the Great Plains plowed under thousands of acres of prairie grass in order to plant more and more wheat and make good money selling it overseas. Farmers elsewhere increased the amount of land they planted too. Soon after the war ended, though, European farmers started planting again and the demand for American crops dropped. When demand dropped, prices for farm goods also dropped, and farmers on the Great Plains fell into debt. Farmers in other parts of the country faced hardship as well.

In the South, farmers had relied on cotton production for many years. When an insect called the boll weevil invaded during the 1890s and then spread across the region in the early twentieth century, it destroyed cotton crops. Many farmers were left with almost nothing to sell and their incomes plummeted. Like the plains farmers, they couldn't make their mortgage payments or pay what they owed for their farming equipment. And at the same time, much of the Southeast and far West experienced a serious drought that caused similar problems in those regions.

As bad as things were for farmers during the 1920s, though, they got even worse in the 1930s. In many parts of the United States, rain simply stopped falling. Each spring, farmers from the Great Lakes to Oregon and North Dakota to Texas got ready to plant, but no rain came.

On the Great Plains, formerly green and gold corn and wheat fields turned to gray dust. Land where sheep or cattle usually grazed did the same. The constant winds that blow across the flat plains picked up the dust and carried it into the sky. Fine, sandy grains of dirt covered everything—indoors as well as out. Still no rain fell. Even today, farmers everywhere worry about getting too little rain or too much rain. They worry about the diseases and insects that can destroy crops. But in the early 1930s, as the dust and dirt continued to swirl around the Great Plains, farmers' and ranchers' worries turned to real fear.

A huge patch of Texas, Oklahoma, Colorado, and Kansas came to be known as the Dust Bowl. Wind sucked fine dirt and dust into terrible black clouds that turned day into night. Farm families saw fences disappear and then whole houses being swallowed by dry, choking dirt as if it were drifting snow. Cattle ranchers watched their livestock root in the dust for nonexistent grass. Without income, ranchers didn't have money to buy feed for their herds. But with so many city people in poverty and not buying expensive food like meat, they couldn't sell the cattle, either. Many slaughtered their herds rather than watch them choke on dust or starve.

On farms and ranches and in towns, gritty dirt got into food and hair and turned white bedsheets brown. Young children and the elderly became ill with "dust pneumonia" as the grit caked their small or weak lungs when they inhaled. Easterners learned how serious the situation was when the sky over Washington, DC, turned dark one day and a fine layer of dirt settled on cars all over the city.[36] Imagine that. A dust storm in Oklahoma had blown thick clouds of dust more than a thousand miles to the nation's capital.

Eventually, hundreds of thousands of farm families on the plains abandoned their once-fertile land and headed west, with no money and little hope of a better future. They wondered how they could have gone from good harvests and bright futures to rock-bottom poverty in such a short time. Most didn't know that the Dust Bowl could have been prevented.

Wild prairie grasses are strong plants that survive drought pretty well and have deep roots that hold the soil in place against the plains winds. Wheat and corn need more water than the wild grasses, and when they are planted in long, straight rows as they were in the 1920s and thirties, their roots can't protect the soil against the wind. Worse, as demand for those crops dropped, farmers stopped planting so much and left big stretches of land empty. Before long, the wind blew away the fertile topsoil, and once the topsoil was gone, nothing would grow. Rich farmland turned to desert.

Franklin Roosevelt hadn't spent time on the Great Plains, but he had seen the effects of drought and poor planting methods. After he was stricken with polio, he'd heard about a place called Warm Springs, Georgia. When he discovered the soothing effects of the naturally warm waters there in 1924, he had a cottage built and visited often. He enjoyed the feeling of freedom he experienced there as the warm waters let him float and swim easily. Roosevelt loved to drive through the Georgia countryside around Warm Springs in the hand-controlled car he'd designed for himself. Off he'd go, stopping to talk with farmers and their families on back roads and country lanes. As he'd always done, he asked questions wherever he went: What crops did people plant? Did

Could There Be Another Dust Bowl?

Drought, wind, and human activity combined to cause the Dust Bowl of the 1930s. Since then, the federal government has supported efforts to educate and encourage farmers to protect the land. But climate change is bringing drier conditions to the Great Plains, and frequent droughts are predicted. During the droughts of the 1950s and 1980s, farmers irrigated their fields with water from the Ogallala Aquifer—a shallow pool of water that lies beneath the plains. But that aquifer does not refill quickly the way some aquifers do, and if it dries up, scientists estimate that it will take six thousand years of rainfall to refill it. Plains farmers are turning to drought-resistant crops; dry farming, where no irrigation is used; and ways of planting that don't disturb the soil as tilling or plowing does. The federal government also pays farmers to leave some land unplanted so natural grasses can renew the soil. Could there be another Dust Bowl? Yes—if climate change brings more frequent severe droughts, if farmers don't continue to use conservation measures, and if government policy does not support agricultural research and conservation efforts.

they rotate crops or fields? Use fertilizer? Plant in straight rows or in curved patterns?

By the time he became president, Roosevelt had learned that Georgia's farmers, like farmers in many other places, had overplanted, plowed in straight rows, and put the same crops on the land year after year. Their soil was damaged. In heavy rain it turned to mud that then dried as hard as cement. In drought, it cracked like the shell on a hardboiled egg. Many farm families in the Southeast, especially African Americans who didn't own their own land and had to rent fields from landowners, couldn't make a living. They finally gave up and moved to northern cities, looking for work and an escape from racism. Houston Pritchett's family was one of the thousands who went north. They left South Carolina in the late twenties when Houston's father decided to move them all to Detroit, where he found a job in an automobile plant—until the Depression hit.[37]

Many of the problems in American agriculture might have been avoided if farmers knew more and used better farming techniques. Human mistakes had caused many of the problems America's forests faced in the 1930s too. For years, timber companies made money by "clear-cutting" trees. They moved their workers and equipment into a big section of forest, cut down all the trees, and then moved on to the next section. Businesses saved money by clear-cutting instead of choosing to cut some trees and not others. They saved even more by abandoning the barren land rather than replanting. But new growth couldn't keep up with what was being cut, and that was dangerous for the future of the forests and the lumber industry. Clear-cutting also created environmental issues.

Tree roots grow deep into the earth and hold the soil in place even on steep hillsides. When the trees on a hill are cut down, rain and wind erode the bare land, causing serious mudslides and rockslides. Trees also help keep the air clean by taking in carbon dioxide and sending out oxygen. Without trees, air pollution increases. And clear-cutting forests destroys the habitats of hundreds of birds and animals, which then die off.

Could anything be done? Some people believed only Mother Nature could make changes in the environment. They didn't accept the research that showed human mistakes were partly to blame for the situation. Others thought it was already too late to repair the damage. But Franklin Roosevelt was optimistic, and he wanted his Civilian Conservation Corps ready to get to work right away.

A recruitment poster for the CCC.

CHAPTER 4

A Miracle of Cooperation

While FDR met with his cabinet at the White House, a young man named Henry Rich looked for work just blocks away. Henry Rich had a friendly, freckled face, curly brown hair, and an ironic name: young Mr. Rich was quite poor. A few weeks before Franklin Roosevelt's inauguration, twenty-five-year-old Henry had left his family home in Durham, North Carolina. He carried a worn guitar and almost no money. Rich made his way 250 cold, hungry miles north to Washington, DC, hoping that the new president would be able to give men like him work. *Any* work. At first Henry had no luck and stood in line for soup and bread like other desperate people. But four weeks after Roosevelt was sworn in, Henry Rich heard the news he'd been waiting for. The president was starting a conservation work program for unemployed young men.

On April 7, 1933, Rich went to the nearest recruiting office in Alexandria, Virginia, just across the Potomac River from Washington, DC. He was determined to get one of the conservation jobs, whatever they were, and he got there early—so early that he was first in line when the office opened for business. Little did he know that he was about to make history that spring morning. When Henry Rich signed his enrollment papers, he became the very first member of the Civilian Conservation Corps.[38]

Within a week, thousands of other young men had joined the CCC, and by June the Civilian Conservation Corps was enrolling nearly fourteen thousand young men around the country every day. Each one received food, a uniform, and about two weeks of training in basic skills and discipline. Soon they'd be sent to work in the CCC camps that were being built everywhere.[39] Nothing like it had ever happened before.

Henry Rich and the rest of the boys lining up to join the CCC didn't ask how the program had come together so quickly. Most couldn't have explained the government's process for establishing programs of any kind. They were simply happy to be employed and fed. But if they had asked how it all happened, they would have learned that it was the work of an extraordinary team of advisers in FDR's cabinet and a Congress ready to pass laws at lightning speed.

At the March 9 meeting, some cabinet members had wondered if the president really meant what he said when he proposed having a half-million young men at work in just weeks. Even though they thought the program sounded good, how would they enroll five hundred thousand recruits in such a short time? Where would the young men come from?

Roosevelt had waved off his advisers' concerns. "You've seen them lining up at the breadlines," he said. "Take them right off the breadline."[40]

But who would supervise these boys, train them, make sure they had food and medical care? Roosevelt told his cabinet secretaries to sort it all out. Fast.

Franklin Roosevelt wasn't afraid of experts. His advisers during the presidential campaign had been called the Brain Trust. FDR wanted advice from professors, leaders of industry, government officials, researchers—anyone with expertise, whether they liked or agreed with him or not. As president, he appointed the best and brightest people he could find to his cabinet. The nine men and one woman who would now lead the departments and agencies of the executive branch of government were very well-equipped for their jobs.

Secretary of Labor Frances Perkins had master's degrees in both sociology and economics. She had spent nearly thirty years improving the lives of working-class people and the poor, part of that time as an adviser to Roosevelt when he was governor of New York. The president trusted Perkins's intelligence and common sense. When he told her to find a way to recruit all those young men in just a few weeks, he didn't doubt for a minute that she would succeed.

That confidence was typical of Roosevelt. He cheerfully demanded quick thinking and a can-do attitude from all his advisers and aides. The day he described his ideas for a civilian conservation project, for example, he said he wanted a bill—the proposed law outlining his plan—that he could present to Congress. That's the way many bills come about. But Roosevelt was in a bigger hurry than most presidents. He wanted that bill before the day was over. That's *not* how it's usually done, but he was serious. The young aides assigned to write the bill worked furiously to get it to him that evening. They would have liked more time, but somehow, they pushed themselves and met the president's deadline.[41]

Next Roosevelt had asked his secretaries of labor, war (now called the secretary of defense), the interior, and agriculture to get together and turn his idea into the reality of tens of thousands of young men working in forests and parks by early summer. The four new cabinet members had just met and hadn't talked about the program or even thought much about it before. But they sat down and got started on what seemed like an impossible task.

FDR had made it clear that Frances Perkins and the Department of Labor would take care of recruiting and enrolling the boys. It wasn't nearly as simple as Roosevelt's suggestion that they just "take them off the breadlines." Only boys whose families were in poverty would be accepted, so Perkins had to be sure of each young man's situation. Most states had agencies working to help unemployed people. Secretary Perkins suggested that her department contact those offices in every state to identify boys whose families most needed help. They'd have to find boys in cities—FDR's first priority—but also in small towns and rural areas. And of course, the department would need to get the word out in newspapers and on the radio. Posters at town halls and post offices might help too. And they'd have to set up offices in cities and towns everywhere, so the boys could get to an office to apply for the program.

What would the boys need once they did enroll?

Obviously, they'd need food, clothes, and shelter right away. Anyone who'd seen the young men in breadlines knew their clothes were practically rags. Those who were living in cardboard boxes or wandering the streets probably hadn't bathed in months. And they all looked stick-thin and hungry.

Secretary of War George Dern had a solution for all this. The Great War had ended fifteen years earlier in 1918, and the army was now much smaller than it had been then. He suggested that the boys could go to vacant military posts as soon as they signed their papers. Barracks, showers, and mess halls at those posts could be made ready very quickly. And piles of surplus tents, cots, blankets, uniforms, and other equipment were collecting dust in army warehouses. The Civilian Conservation Corps could put all those things to good use, at least as a start. The young men could spend a week or two adapting to living together and following orders and then go by bus or train to the new camps where they'd be working.

Perkins had pointed out that "an awful lot of these unemployed people have heart trouble, varicose veins, and everything else."[42] She was right. Malnutrition, dirty living conditions, and the cold took their toll even on young people, who should have been at the peak of health. Many of them wheezed with asthma. Others were tired and weak from the hookworms that lived in their intestines and stole whatever protein they ate. Some suffered with crooked, bowed leg bones from rickets because they didn't get enough calcium. These boys hadn't seen a doctor or dentist in years. Some had never had any kind of medical care. Health insurance was a new idea in the 1930s, and very few people could afford it. Everyone else paid for each doctor visit or hospital stay or operation in cash. The boys Roosevelt wanted to hire didn't have money, so they simply went without medical care, even when they were sick or injured.

Dern had a solution for that, too. Army doctors could give the boys medical exams before they were accepted into the CCC. They needed to be able to work hard, and sick men couldn't do that. Also, young men with tuberculosis or other contagious diseases couldn't live in close quarters with healthy young men. Everyone might get sick.

The cabinet would still need to figure out how to get camps set up in just weeks. Those old army tents and cots would have to do until barracks could be built. And how would they feed the recruits and camp officers once they arrived at their work sites? Think about all the food they'd need. A camp of two hundred or more young men eating a couple of sandwiches for lunch would require at least forty loaves of bread and whatever went inside it, plus twenty-five or thirty gallons of milk to wash it down. The

Health Insurance Today

Health insurance came about in the late 1920s, when private companies first offered health insurance *policies*. The idea was that a person could buy a policy and the company would then pay the cost of that person's medical care. Very few people at the time could afford to buy policies, though most people want health insurance. After all, even very healthy people can have a serious and costly illness or accident. Today governments in nearly all wealthy countries make sure that everyone in the country has health insurance or government-provided health care. That is not the case in the United States. During the

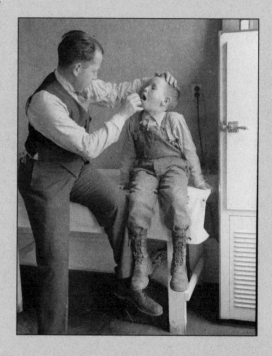

1950s, American employers offered to share the cost of insurance with employees. Currently, about half of all Americans have health insurance through an employer. Another third are covered by Medicare or Medicaid—tax-supported health insurance for the elderly and very poor. But about 15 percent of Americans do not have health insurance and are far more likely to lose their homes and savings to medical costs than insured people.[150] The percentage of uninsured Americans decreased between 2010 and 2016 but started increasing again in 2017.[151]

president had asked for more than a thousand camps by July 4. Someone would have to deliver over forty thousand loaves of bread and about twenty-five thousand gallons of milk to remote areas for every lunch every day. And that doesn't count breakfast, dinner, and anything else.

A lot of needy boys had been hanging around on street corners and getting into trouble for months or even years—they were going to require discipline and structure as well as food and shelter. Since army officers had experience leading men of all sorts, Dern pointed out, it might be best to have the army run the camps as well as the training centers. And the CCC could hire reserve military officers who had lost their regular jobs to take charge of the boys. That would be what the president had called "killing two birds with one stone." He'd like that.

Finally, as secretary of the interior, Harold Ickes oversaw the National Park Service. He would recommend and supervise park projects in every state. He'd have to get suggestions and requests from state officials around the country. Henry Wallace, the secretary of agriculture and in charge of the Forest Service, would identify the biggest needs in forestry and soil projects.

Getting the Civilian Conservation Corps up and running didn't feel quite as impossible by the time the meeting was over. It made sense to share the responsibility among four government departments—that might be the only way to get the job done quickly. Even so, it wasn't the usual way of doing things.

Government agencies then (and now) had a terrible reputation when it came to working together. Historians have called the cooperation among departments in the spring of 1933 "miraculous"[43] and a lesson in what government *ought* to be able to accomplish. For young men like Henry Rich, though, this wasn't a civics or government lesson. It meant the difference between earning a living and going hungry.

No matter how talented and cooperative the members of Roosevelt's cabinet were, though, the executive branch of government alone couldn't make the CCC a reality. Presidents can suggest programs, but only Congress can provide the money to build and run those programs. Before Henry Rich and all the others could sign up, Congress had to pass a law establishing the Civilian Conservation Corps.

On March 21, twelve days after the cabinet members had met, President Roosevelt presented a list of proposals to Congress. The one he was most determined to get approved and funded quickly was the Civilian Conservation Corps. Roosevelt invited key legislators to the White House, where he could talk to them about it personally. Then he sent Secretary of Labor Frances Perkins and other officials to the Capitol to answer Congress's questions.

Wearing her trademark black dress and hat, Perkins marched into the United States Capitol as if female cabinet officers testified in front of Congress every day. They didn't. After all, she was the first. She'd had doubts about the CCC in the beginning, and she knew some members of Congress would object. But Perkins had become convinced of the program's value and was ready to defend it.[44]

Many members of Congress represented districts where factory, mine, and mill workers lived and voted. They worried that the Corps' low wages of one dollar a day would encourage business owners to lower regular workers' wages. Perkins told them that was wrong. The Civilian Conservation Corps was not offering regular jobs. It was offering relief for decent but poor young men. Their salaries could not be compared to factory workers' wages because the boys would be given housing, clothing, and food paid for by the government. That added up to quite a bit more than a dollar a day.[45] The CCC would have no impact at all on what regular workers earned.

Other representatives feared that the CCC would be like the communist takeover of jobs in the Soviet Union. They'd heard about the end of economic freedom as the government there decided what factories would make and what prices they would charge. Those representatives wanted nothing to do with a government-controlled economy. No, Perkins said. The CCC would be absolutely nothing like communism. The United States government wasn't going to tell factory owners anything about what to make or how much to charge. The US was a market economy and would stay that way. The government would simply put needy boys to work on necessary and worthwhile projects that no business would want to do. Businesses exist to make money—nobody was going to make money building wilderness parks with no admission fees or planting trees to block the wind on the Great

Plains. That was why the government needed to take on that kind of project. It would be a win for all sides.

Roosevelt's army chief of staff testified that recruits would not be taught anything at all about national defense or weapons. The CCC wasn't military training, as some people had said it was. The

The Boy Scouts

The Boy Scouts were founded in England in 1908 and in the United States in 1910 (the Girl Scouts were founded in the US in 1912). The Boy Scouts' goal was to help boys develop good citizenship, learn outdoor skills, and behave in a kind, courteous, helpful way. Franklin Roosevelt first supported the Boy Scouts in 1915. He was the assistant secretary of the navy at the time and served on the Special Committee on Nautical Scouting.[152] Now called Sea Scouting, the program teaches boating skills and water safety. Later Roosevelt worked to establish Boy Scout camps in New York State. As president, FDR invited the Boy Scouts of America to hold their first jamboree—an enormous gathering of scouts—in Washington, DC. Today about four million boys and girls in the US participate in scouting.

boys would be no more military than Boy Scouts. The army simply had the know-how to oversee the boys and the camps.

The questions continued.

So did the answers.

Just days later, the Emergency Conservation Work Act passed in both the House and the Senate, and President Roosevelt signed it into law on March 31. FDR had gotten his conservation corps proposed, planned, and passed in under four weeks.

Ask anyone today if Congress could pass a law that quickly. *Impossible.* But Roosevelt had bipartisan support in Congress— that is, support from both his fellow Democrats *and* from many of his Republican opponents. Yes, he had support from members of the opposition. They believed that the crisis was so severe they had to let the president try his ideas. As one Missouri Republican said, "I do not like to see us go along on a project such as this, but I do like the way the President of the U.S. is trying to meet this emergency, and I have gone along with him."[46]

That miracle of speed and cooperation allowed Henry Rich and boys like him to enroll in the CCC very quickly. One article said that newscasters on the radio "could, for a change, say, 'There's good news tonight.'"[47]

The good news of the Emergency Conservation Work Act included one provision that only a few people knew about at first. It was a miracle within a miracle. Oscar De Priest of Illinois, the only African American member of Congress in 1933, had attached an antidiscrimination amendment to the bill. The CCC would not discriminate based on "race, color, creed, or criminal records." Congress voted to accept the amendment—something no one would have expected at the time. The amendment allowed young African Americans like Houston Pritchett of Detroit the chance to change their lives the way Henry Rich did. That kind of opportunity was very rare in the 1930s.

Congress quickly moved on to other proposals from the president, while young men in Virginia filled out their paperwork and headed for Fort Washington in nearby Maryland. The fort, on the banks of the Potomac River just south of Washington, DC, had been built to protect the city in 1809. But in 1933, it was used only by a ceremonial unit and had plenty of room for CCC recruits. The young men spent the next two weeks eating three solid meals a day for the first time in quite a while. They also exercised to build energy and strength and learned to follow orders. It felt good to belong somewhere, and good to have a full belly and tired muscles at the end of the day. Soon the nearly two hundred young men at Fort Washington were ready to get to work.

In the meantime, Roosevelt's advisers rushed to sort out all the details of getting the camps ready. The key decision was up to the president: Where would the first recruits go once their brief training was finished?

Two days after Henry signed his papers, President and Mrs. Roosevelt, Interior Secretary Harold Ickes, and a small group of advisers traveled to Virginia's Blue Ridge Mountains, seventy-five miles west of Washington. Conservation groups had been trying to establish a national park in the Blue Ridge for several years. They'd succeeded in convincing Congress to authorize Shenandoah National Park, but they'd run into problems acquiring enough money to buy all the land for the park. That had slowed them down. Once the economy collapsed in 1929, the whole project looked like an impossible dream.

Now FDR headed for a fishing camp along the Rapidan River in the Blue Ridge Mountains. The camp had belonged to President Herbert Hoover and his wife, who loved the peace and quiet there. When Hoover left office, he and Mrs. Hoover had donated the cottage compound to the government for future presidents to enjoy.[48] Roosevelt didn't plan to go fishing and couldn't easily stay in the camp's cottages, but he wanted to see the area he'd heard so much about. (Today Rapidan Camp is part of Shenandoah National Park, and presidents have a country retreat at Camp David in Maryland.)

Harold Ickes was eager to see the Blue Ridge too. Like his boss, he was a conservationist and had even campaigned for FDR's distant cousin Theodore Roosevelt years earlier. Ickes believed that people could enjoy the nation's natural resources and protect them at the same time. That was the point of national parks. Now, as secretary of the interior, Harold Ickes could try out his ideas. He was determined to restore the places Teddy Roosevelt had loved—parks like Yellowstone in Wyoming, Yosemite in California, and Grand Canyon in Arizona. He planned to ask for new parks too, especially in the East. Most Americans lived between the Atlantic Ocean and the Mississippi River in the 1930s, but there was only one national park in the whole region—far from most of the population, on the coast of Maine.

Like Roosevelt, Ickes believed all people could benefit from time spent in nature's most beautiful and impressive places. Visitors standing on the rim of the Grand Canyon tended to whisper. Whole families stood awed by the world's tallest trees. More parks would allow millions of people to share that kind of experience.

When Roosevelt and Ickes looked east from the top of the Blue Ridge Mountains on that early April day, they saw farms and fields spread like a patchwork quilt across the rolling hills. On the western side of the ridge lay the Shenandoah Valley, covered at that time of year by an ocean of lacy pink apple blossoms. Drought and tree disease had left brown and gray scars in the valleys and on the mountains. Still, the president and his aides felt like they were a million miles from the complicated battles going on in Congress or the stacks of letters begging them for help in these hard times. Here, they could take a deep breath before going back to fight the nation's crises. Roosevelt and Ickes agreed that every American should be able to feel the same way.

FDR decided that day that his conservation program would get started right here in Virginia. Recruits could improve the national forests already there and get going on the Corps' first major project. The CCC would turn this land into Shenandoah National Park.

An example of a CCC camp in Breen Burney Camp in Lassen National Forest, California.

CHAPTER 5

Into the Woods

In the early light of a chilly April morning, Henry Rich and the other recruits at Fort Washington gathered their few belongings together. Some simply tied small bundles with string and were ready to get on a bus for the Blue Ridge Mountains. They ate a five a.m. breakfast and picked up bag lunches to take with them. Ten days of training didn't sound like much, yet most of the boys felt stronger and healthier than they had when they enrolled. They were still getting used to barracks living, but it was certainly better than living on the streets. And while some were a bit nervous about going out into the woods to work, they were glad to have jobs. Real, paying jobs.

The buses were expected at Fort Washington at six o'clock that morning, but six came and went with no sign of them. The boys waited and then waited some more. Still no buses. Someone somewhere had made a mistake. By the time the Greyhound charters pulled in, many of the recruits were already getting hungry for lunch. They carried their bologna sandwiches on board and settled down for the long ride to the George Washington National Forest, just west of the Blue Ridge Mountains, where Shenandoah National Park was going to be built.

The trip along the winding country roads (interstate highways weren't built until the 1950s) was slow and bumpy. As the buses snaked around turns, the dark, oily smell of engine exhaust was enough to give some fellows queasy stomachs. The smell of stale bologna sandwiches couldn't have helped. When they finally approached their destination late in the day, the drivers realized the buses couldn't climb all the way up the narrow, rutted mountain road. They dropped the boys at the foot of a long hill and headed home.[49]

Shadows lengthened as the two hundred weary young men trudged up the old dirt logging path. Their sandwiches were now a distant memory, and they had no more food with them. Some were anxious to see their new home; others must have wondered what they'd gotten themselves into. The boys felt proud to be part of the first Civilian Conservation Corps camp in the country. But when they got to the top of the road, they didn't know what to think. There was no *camp* at Camp Roosevelt. As George Dant, one of Henry's camp mates, described it, "There was nothing but open sky and one single canvas-covered army truck in a ten-acre clearing."[50]

Government workers assigned to organize the CCC from their office in Washington had done their best. But they'd only been on the job for three weeks, and that wasn't nearly enough time to have barracks or a dining hall or a bathhouse built at any of the proposed camps. Still, the boys should have seen a whole convoy of trucks in that clearing—moving vans filled with food, tents, blankets, and everything else two hundred recruits would need. The one truck that was there carried cots. No food, no water, no blankets or tents. Just cots. The men set them up in the wet field. At least they could sit on something dry while they waited for help. Apparently, the convoy had gotten lost.

Before long, the camp cook and the mess officer (the person in charge of the food operation) drove into the clearing in their own cars. They found two hundred bedraggled, hungry young men sitting in the gathering darkness without even a battery-powered lamp or a jug of water. The two men got back in their cars and went in search of the missing convoy.

It soon grew too dark for the boys to see a thing, darker than many city boys had ever experienced. Picture a cloudy night with no moon or stars. Then take away all electricity, streetlights, neighborhood houses, and cars. That kind of darkness can be frightening. And there were noises, too. For young men used to trolley bells and car horns, the animal yelps and howls in the distance sounded like something out of a radio horror show.

Thunder rumbled. Then lightning flashed and hard rain slapped the ground. Some boys had rain jackets in their bags. Those who didn't felt the cold water soak through their clothes and drip down their faces and necks. At that moment, they were just as miserable as they'd been on their own. A few had second thoughts about joining the CCC.

At long last, a second truck rolled into the clearing, carrying lanterns and flashlights. Lights wouldn't keep anyone dry, but at least the boys could see one another. Next, the mess officer and cook returned. They hadn't found the convoy, but they had managed to buy every cooked hot dog and hamburger in every tiny restaurant they came across. Imagine how good even cold dogs and burgers tasted at that point.[51]

It was nearly midnight when the rest of the trucks finally rumbled up the road. As tired as everyone was by then, they had to unload the trucks, set up rows of huge tents, and find the blankets they all needed. There was hardly time for some sleep before they had to be up again. But the rain had stopped, and that was good news.

Before long, the rain started again and continued off and on over the next few weeks. It didn't rain all day every day, but it never stopped long enough for anything to dry out. Camp Roosevelt turned into a sea of soupy muck. Cooks fought to keep fires burning while water dripped off tarps onto their outdoor cookstoves. The boys slipped and slid in mud as they hauled drinking and cooking water from a stream. They took baths farther down the same stream but often had a hard time getting dry and dressed before the rain came again. And learning to relieve themselves in the open trenches they dug some distance from the rest of the camp wasn't easy to begin with. Using the trenches without sliding in the mud was a real challenge. Somehow, though, they managed to start work on their first assignments, building roads and bridges into the forest.

Conditions at the president's first CCC camp were rough, but most recruits stuck it out. After all, they had shelter of sorts and food, even if the food was a bit soggy at times. Besides, the boys liked feeling they were part of something worthwhile. It would take time and a lot of hard work to build miles of roads and however many bridges and other structures they were asked to build, but they had signed up because they wanted to work. A little rain wasn't going to derail them. The Civilian Conservation Corps had become reality, and the boys had given it a slogan: We Can Take It!

Woody Wilson had been looking at the Blue Ridge Mountains all his life. Fifty miles west of Herndon, they hung like misty blue clouds above the hills, disappearing in gray rain, then reappearing—still misty blue—against a robin's-egg sky. Woody could have told the president and secretary of the interior about the streaks of purple and pink that framed the mountains at sunset, and the curtains of black that covered them when a storm moved in. What he couldn't have told them was how much working on those mountains would change his life.

On May 1—just three weeks after Henry Rich signed up—Walker Woodrow Wilson entered the Civilian Conservation Corps recruiting office at Camp Humphreys, Virginia (now called Fort Belvoir), about thirty miles from his home. He didn't often travel that far, but he wasn't going to miss the chance for a job. Neither were the other young men standing in line.

Some of the boys had read articles about the CCC in local newspapers. Others heard announcements on the radio or saw posters at town halls and post offices, just as Perkins and her recruitment team had planned. A lot of young men got the news as Henry Rich did—from other young men. Already, word of the Civilian Conservation Corps was everywhere.

Woody gave his name as Woodrow Wilson, dropping the Walker. He had turned eighteen in January and said that when he worked, his occupation was farming. He'd never lived on a farm, but Herndon was a farming community, and Woody had taken odd jobs wherever he could.[52] Why did he say he worked in farming when he didn't really work much at all? Most likely, Woody didn't want to sound as though he'd never worked. He didn't want to sound like a do-nothing loafer. It was embarrassing to be unemployed at his age, even if it wasn't his fault.

All the boys were in the same situation. But the fact was that no one who'd had a job in the last six months could apply to the Civilian Conservation Corps. That was one of the rules. Recruits had to be unmarried and between eighteen and twenty-five years of age as well. Some boys, desperate for work, lied about their age and got away with it. Albert Willett, one of fourteen children in his family, managed to enroll when he was not yet fifteen.[53] Did the recruiter really believe he was eighteen? No, and his company commander didn't either. Willett simply didn't look eighteen or close to it. But a lot of recruiters and officers didn't question someone like Albert Willett too carefully. No one wanted to turn down a boy who was going hungry at home or who didn't have a home at all.

Woody filled in the personal details his application asked for. He measured five feet seven and one-half inches tall, average at the time. He had blue eyes, a ruddy complexion, and no serious illnesses. Yes, his father was unemployed and they needed help. Yes, he could read and write and had gone to school, but only through the eighth grade. Before he knew it, he was in line for a medical exam.[54]

The boys removed their shirts so doctors could listen to their lungs and hearts. They were a bony bunch with ribs sticking out. Many had stooped shoulders and grayish skin. Some had the ailments Frances Perkins had worried about. And most looked like they hadn't had a good meal in a long time.

Doctors rejected boys whose health was too poor, but they often tried to get help for them if they could, especially those who had tuberculosis or other serious diseases and needed to go to a hospital. The young men behind them in line worried that they might be rejected too. But Woody passed his physical and signed his enrollment papers. His pay? Thirty dollars a month—one dollar a day for eight hours of digging trenches, chopping down trees, or building roads. In today's money, that would be about eighteen dollars a day or just over two dollars an hour. Signing the contract meant he agreed to that low salary. He signed, just like everyone else who could.

Where Were the Women?

During the 1930s, most middle-class people assumed that men supported their families financially and women took care of the home and children. During the Great Depression, very little attention was given to creating jobs for women, even though millions of women had always supported their families through paid work. Frances Perkins was a good example. With her husband ill and unable to work, her income supported the family, something Perkins rarely mentioned. In fact, she didn't often talk about her husband and daughter at all. She worried that if people knew she was married and a mother, she would lose her job and her family would fall into poverty. She and First Lady Eleanor Roosevelt worked together to create a female corps somewhat like the CCC. Its focus would be teaching women skills that could lead to jobs in their local communities. The program never gained very much support, and there were only ninety camps around the country serving just 8,500 women before it ended.[153]

He also agreed to the CCC's requirement that twenty-five of his thirty dollars be sent to his family each month, leaving just five dollars for him to keep. That was fine with Woody and the other boys too. The young men wanted to help their families survive, and twenty-five dollars could buy enough bread, milk, oatmeal, beans, and chicken to feed a family of four for a month. They were happy and proud to send that money home. They wouldn't need much money in the Corps, anyway. They had a cot, work clothes, and three meals a day waiting for them. That was plenty. Besides, they were getting a chance to have more adventure than they'd ever had before and would even learn skills they could put to use in other jobs later on.

Woody took an oath pledging to stay in the Corps for six months and obey the rules. He filled out a card telling his parents how to contact him, and it was done: He was now a member of the Civilian Conservation Corps, Company 334. Recruits didn't even need to go home and pack extra underwear—if they owned any. The Corps would supply it.

The boys of Company 334 spent the next two weeks as the first group of enrollees had—eating, exercising, and learning to take orders. Then they headed west to Shenandoah National Park Camp Number One, Skyland. Like Camp Roosevelt, there were no buildings yet at Skyland, but the boys did find huge tents lined up across a flat, rocky meadow. Barracks would come later.

Slopes patched with thick green forest rose behind the tents.

But bare earth and erosion marred sections of the hillsides. Stands of lifeless, leafless trees covered hills below. Their gray limbs looked eerie in the middle of spring and made the mountains seem a bit scary. Recruits who'd grown up in the area had a name for those stands of tree skeletons: ghost forests. Clearly, turning such a place into a beautiful national park was going to take imagination and an awful lot of sweat.

The new enrollees settled ten to a tent, their army cots closer together than many of them found comfortable. Woody had never known much privacy in a large family with a small house and no indoor toilet. But this was something else, especially when heavy spring rains left the canvas tents musty with mildew and early summer heat added the salty, sweaty smell of ten close bodies to the air. It took some getting used to. Living and working with recruits from many different backgrounds also took getting used to.

Mountain boys, for example, recognized the sounds of screech owls and bobcats in the night. They knew it was a blight of devastating fungus that turned beautiful chestnut trees into ghosts. Some had grown up on farms very near the parkland, and others lived deep in the backwoods and had never learned to read. Most of the recruits at Skyland were from Virginia, but the mountain boys had their own distinct way of speaking and could be hard to understand.

City boys from Richmond, Virginia, or Washington, DC, didn't sound like the mountain boys. They didn't dress the same way either, wearing fedoras instead of soft felt hats. These young men had grown up hearing their close-by neighbors argue or laugh. They could tell what those families were having for dinner because the odors drifted into their own houses or apartments. But most city boys had had very little experience with the great outdoors.

Then there were the recruits who came from the Tidewater on Virginia's Atlantic coast. They'd grown up watching the tides and scanning the far-off horizon for storm clouds in a place where some people farmed and watermen spent long, hard days crabbing, fishing, and oystering. Mountains made the Tidewater recruits feel a little claustrophobic and uneasy. The steep hills and trees were beautiful, but not at all like the wide-open wetlands and fields they knew. Yet as different from one another as the Virginia enrollees were, they shared a common distrust of the recruits from Pennsylvania, who had their own accents and ideas.

Woody was a Virginian, but he wasn't a mountain man or a waterman. He wasn't a city boy either. He was just a small-town kid who had seen the mountains, liked to fish, and sometimes went to the city to listen to bluegrass. He was also easygoing, and a little ribbing about how much he ate or being the baby of his family didn't bother him. He loved to laugh and tell a good joke (which he called a story) and maybe even play a small prank—but never a nasty one. Woody Wilson didn't have a mean bone in his body. His sisters-in-law called him "sweet," something he might not have wanted the other recruits to know.[55] That good nature made his transition to camp life smooth. Some boys had a harder time living with fellows who looked or sounded different. It might take a while, but they'd have to learn to get along if they were going to make it in the CCC. The same was true at all the other camps springing up in Virginia and around the country.

In just weeks, boys were adjusting to camp life and their fellow camp mates in every state in the nation. Americans had started talking about the Civilian Conservation Corps. They called it "Roosevelt's Tree Army," though recruits would do far more than plant trees. Eventually, the young men of the CCC would tackle over two hundred different kinds of jobs.

The president couldn't have been happier.

CHAPTER 6

What Will They Do,
Mr. President?

Woody and the rest of the boys in the Blue Ridge were proud that they were going to build a national park. But many of them had never actually seen a park of any kind, and they wondered what kind of work they'd be doing. The boys weren't the only ones with questions.

Back at the original planning meeting on March 9, cabinet member Frances Perkins had expressed her worry about pulling young men from breadlines and taking them to the nation's forests to "turn them loose," as she said. Most cabinet members shared her feelings. Finally Perkins asked the president what everyone wanted to know. "What are they going to do when they get to the woods?"[56]

It was a good question. Roosevelt wanted the boys to build bridges and dams, renew forests and soil, and construct parks. Perkins and the others knew that kind of work was the program's goal. But what *exactly* would thousands of untrained, uneducated boys do as part of that work? What would any one boy do to help build a bridge or repair a forest or construct a park? That would be up to the experts designing each project—professionals such as engineers, landscape architects, and foresters. The boys in the earliest camps would be assigned their specific jobs soon after they arrived.

Skyland wasn't the only CCC camp planned for the area that was going to become Shenandoah National Park. Eventually, ten camps would be up and working in the 160,000-acre park. It would be a small park compared to a place like Yellowstone, which is more than ten times bigger. But let's do some math. Today, many houses in suburban neighborhoods are built on lots of about one-quarter of one acre. That means Shenandoah National Park was the equivalent of 640,000 neighborhood houses and their yards.

The land ran in a long, narrow strip five miles east to west and one hundred miles north to south. Picture a skinny strip of land hugging the backbone of the Blue Ridge Mountains. There would be plenty of room for hiking and camping, but the main attraction was going to be Skyline Drive, a road etched into the ridge of the mountains—something Herbert Hoover had suggested when he spent time there. Such a road would mean that people who couldn't hike or camp could still enjoy the beauty and wonder of the wilderness.

Before the construction could begin, the boys had to make the land ready. That was going to be a big job with a number of challenges. For one thing, most of the land that was to be the park wasn't wilderness at all. Much of it had been farmed, grazed, or timbered for two hundred years. The idea was to turn the area back into what it was before all that—to re-create a wilderness. The story was the same for many proposed CCC park projects in other parts of the country. In those places, the men of the Corps weren't going to put parks in the woods; they were going to put woods in the parks.

Another problem was that several hundred families still lived on land that now belonged to the park. Some farm families hadn't been able to make a good living for a long time and had sold their property to the federal government without hesitation. They moved off the mountain soon after the project was first proposed. Others were torn. Most of those who owned the land they lived on needed the money they were offered, but they resented being forced to move. Moving would mean giving up the mountains they loved and the way of life they had always known. And they didn't want the houses the government promised to build for them in a new community nearby. Then there were the families who rented the land they farmed or who worked as tenant farmers on someone else's land or simply lived on land no one was using. The government wasn't going to give them any money for land they didn't own, and most had to accept one of the new houses if they weren't going to be homeless.

Hundreds of other mountain folk didn't want to leave no matter what the government offered. They weren't wealthy at all, but they had decent, productive farms and they had sued in court to

People of the Blue Ridge

The people who lived on the land that became Shenandoah National Park did not fit any one description of "mountain folk," and they were not the hillbillies that many people imagined they were: Some landowners in the Blue Ridge had college degrees and were very well off. The majority of residents had little education, but they weren't nearly as poor as a lot of people in cities at the time. They often lived in log houses with gardens outside their doors and ate a variety of fruits and vegetables year-round (they preserved and stored food for the winter). Families had chickens, a cow, and a hog or two as well. Most were healthy and independent and liked living in the sparsely populated area.[154] However, times were getting hard for many as the chestnut trees died off and the land grew dry and less fertile. Even so, hundreds of people remained bitter long after they were forced to move out to make way for park construction. The Department of the Interior did allow a number of elderly residents to stay in their homes for the rest of their lives. The last of the mountain people was Annie Shenk. She lived in the house she had shared with her husband, about a mile from park headquarters, for over thirty years after he passed away. She was ninety-two when she died in 1979.[155]

keep their land and houses. The courts ruled against them, saying that the government could take their land and require them to move (this is called the right of *eminent domain*).[57] The people who were still on the mountain as Woody and the other recruits arrived had ignored the court order to leave. Now it was time to force those people out.

CCC recruit Preston Breedon knew about the arguments and court cases over the land. He'd grown up in a log cabin along a road that eventually became part of Skyline Drive. His family was one of those who sold their small, poor farm and moved down the mountain. They went to live with Preston's grandmother. Now Preston had been assigned to a camp and a project on the very land that had been his family's farm. When recruits were told to burn the Breedon cabin to the ground to make way for park construction, Preston Breedon found himself helping to destroy his own home.[58]

The CCC recruits understood that the mountain people were being paid for their land or given new places to live, but some young men still found it difficult to set fire to cabins and farmhouses or tear down fences and barns. Those places weren't *their* homes, but a number of boys knew what it felt like when a family was forced out of its house. It had happened to them when their parents couldn't pay their mortgage or rent.

Fortunately, Woody wasn't asked to destroy anyone's house or tear down any barns. He worked on a road crew. Construction of

Skyline Drive had started two years earlier under a private company, but the road was far from complete. Some of the work had been done badly, and the poor workmanship resulted in serious erosion under and alongside the road and caused dangerous rockslides. The road had to be built again, and built right.

The government hired engineers to plan and oversee the new construction. Woody and dozens of other young men with picks, shovels, and a few pieces of machinery reshaped and softened the sharp slopes where the road cut through the mountainside. They laid stone gutters to slow the rainwater that washed earthen walls away. They built temporary log fences along curves where cars might slide right over the cliffs. Visitors to the park would probably never notice that kind of work. But the young men worked on more visible projects too.

Park planners wanted people to be able to safely pause and appreciate the magnificent views from Skyline Drive. They brought in landscape architects—designers of outdoor spaces—to design overlooks or pullouts at the most scenic places along the road. Visitors could stop their cars to look, snap pictures, and drink in the natural beauty without blocking traffic or risking accidents.

At many of the overlook sites, enrollees climbed partway down the embankment or drop-off on one side of the road and built a framework using ghost forest timber. The framework acted as a gigantic basket reaching up toward the road above. More recruits used picks and shovels to pull dirt and rock down from the upward slope on the other side of the road. Then workers shoveled the dirt and rocks into wheelbarrows and dumped it into the waiting basket framework. The tons of dirt and rock formed a new piece of mountain—a platform strong enough to support people, cars, and even buses. Finally, the boys planted trees and shrubs on and around the platforms. When the plants grew and spread, the new pullouts looked as if they had been a natural part of the earth forever.[59]

The landscape architects also designed guard walls using the beautiful gray stone found in the mountains. The CCC boys dug the stones from the ground, hauled them in wheelbarrows to where the walls were being built, and set them in place one at a time, carefully fitting them together. Slowly, those rocks became the low stone walls Skyline Drive is still known for. The work often left the men tired and sore at the end of the day, but Woody Wilson later said it was the most rewarding work he ever did. It was work he could be proud of, work he'd show his children decades later. Woody Wilson helped turn Skyline Drive into one of the most scenic roads in the country.

As the road crews Woody worked with built walls and overlooks and the road itself, other crews got busy on an astonishing number of jobs. Obviously, the ghost forests had to go. The dead trees were ugly and likely to fall in high winds. That could be dangerous. Even more dangerous was the fire hazard they created. Dead trees get very dry, and despite the early spring rains, Virginia was still in the midst of a serious drought in the summer of 1933. A lightning strike to one of the chestnut skeletons could set off a forest fire very close to the boys' camps or the nearby towns. So recruits headed out day after day to clear the hills of the dead trees.

They learned to use two-man handsaws—longer than the recruits were tall—to bring down the biggest ghosts. Real cooperation and team effort went into perfecting the rhythm that kept those saws humming through trunks over four feet in diameter. Other boys perched on steep hillsides, searching for solid footholds near the smaller trees before they swung their heavy axes. A misstep could mean a bad gash or worse.

Still other crews went after gooseberry shrubs, fast-growing bushes that produce edible fruit but choke other plants if they aren't contained. "We were told to go out and pull all the goose-berries up, hang them up in trees with their roots up to air dry," one recruit said. "We would come back in about ninety days and put them in piles and burn them."[60] Some teams wore long sleeves and gloves even on the hottest days as they dug out thorny bushes and destructive brambles. Many boys built muscle hauling away fallen timber and debris.

Despite all this backbreaking labor, however, the work had hardly begun. The men of the CCC still had to create a wilder-ness in Shenandoah National Park. But bit by bit, they were mak-ing that possible—just as President Roosevelt envisioned.

Section after section of land was made ready for the next step in the project. Landscape architects soon began directing the planting of what amounted to a garden of two hundred thousand acres. They chose to bring back plants like mountain laurel and other native species that had grown in the Blue Ridge generations earlier. They got some of those plants from other parts of the region and had recruits clear land for nurseries—places to grow plants—near the town of Front Royal at the northern end of the park. On flat, fertile plots, city boys who had never watered a houseplant learned to coax tiny seedlings into saplings and nurture small sprigs into lush shrubs that would be planted elsewhere in the park.[61]

The landscape experts also planned to move existing trees and bushes from one part of the park to another. Recruits who arrived knowing nothing at all about trees or shrubs now trudged through the hills and valleys, identifying wild dogwood, rhododendron, and other native species. They dug up the plants they found, carefully preserving their roots, and then moved and replanted them on the slopes where the ghost forests had stood. Other plants went onto the hillsides alongside the road, where their roots would help keep the soil in place. More bushes and small trees went to the former pastures and farm fields and to the clearings where mountain children had played just months earlier.

The men worked in teams to move the bigger trees, some as tall as fifteen feet. Rope lines of thirty men fought giant tug-of-war battles with eight-foot root balls. When they won, they dragged the trees and the root balls through ravines they had dug. The ravines made paths to wooden ramps that led onto truck beds.

Once the men got the trees to their new sites, they dragged them back off the trucks and wrestled them into waiting holes twice the size of the root ball.

The enrollees planted hundreds of thousands of trees and shrubs throughout the park, one plant at a time. Slowly but surely, a forest rose where farmland, dead trees, and eroded land had been. The boys of the Civilian Conservation Corps weren't called the "Tree Army" for nothing.

Still, there was more to do. Planners hoped to make the park available for all kinds of people. They wanted to see thousands of visitors enjoying themselves there every year. Some would come to hike, fish, or camp. But many would come simply for the scenery. Couples with children would picnic and elderly people would come to get away from city heat. Those visitors would need running water, restrooms, telephones in case of emergency (this was decades before cell phones), and more. That meant that water pipes had to be brought in and telephone lines had to be laid in trenches stretching up the mountainside.

The work of laying those lines required large teams of strong men. Recruit Arthur Emory, a big young man, was assigned to one of those teams. As he said, "I signed up to be a cook and they handed me a shovel."[62] Emory and hundreds of others dug trenches one foot wide and three feet deep. The huge rocks they pulled out of the ground as they dug went to the guard walls. If they hit bedrock—the solid rock under the surface—they used jackhammers, whose bone-jarring, earsplitting vibrations left a worker feeling and hearing the machine long after he'd shut it down.

Once the trenches were ready, the telephone lines had to be put into them and then buried. Telephone lines were made of several strands of cable wrapped in lead for protection, which made them very heavy. The boys spaced themselves eight or ten feet apart. Each of them slung a one-hundred-pound section of the long cable over his shoulder and followed the man in front up the mountain. Most enrollees wouldn't have been strong enough for that kind of work when they first joined the CCC, but after a month or so of good food and exercise they were.

A variety of jobs meant work for other teams. Carpentry crews cut the wood from the downed ghost trees and soaked it in water, a process that made the wood stronger. The young men then used the wood to make shingles, picnic shelters, tables, and fence posts. They cut big notches into some of the widest lumber, which other crews then stacked like giant Lincoln Logs to support the new bridges being built across streams and ravines. Regardless of which team they were on, a shower and a hearty meal sounded very good when those men returned to camp every afternoon.

The work would have been a lot easier if the men had used machines instead of hand tools for more of it. Why didn't the CCC have more machines to get the job done? For one thing, very few recruits had any experience with machinery. It takes some training to use even simple hand tools like hammers and saws, and much more training for power tools or big machinery. Machines can be dangerous even for experienced workers, and the CCC wanted to keep the boys safe. Moreover, buying enough machinery for all the CCC projects in the country would have been extremely costly. And transporting that machinery to the out-of-the-way sites where the boys were working would be both difficult and expensive, if it could be done at all. Besides, doing the projects by hand required far more workers than using machines, and a major goal of the CCC was putting as many young men to work as possible.

The government supplied some needed machinery, like bulldozers and backhoes and so on, and also supplied every camp with the hand tools the recruits would need for the kind of work they were assigned. Picks, sledgehammers, handsaws, and axes were commonly used. The boys used shovels for so many tasks—from digging latrines to burying telephone lines and putting out forest fires—that a simple shovel became a proud symbol of the Corps.

The majority of enrollees in the Shenandoah National Park camps worked in construction or in clearing the land and planting trees and shrubs. But some provided the support needed to keep hundreds of young men at their jobs. A recruit who was good with numbers, for example, might help keep track of supplies. And young men with mechanical skills were needed to maintain trucks and equipment. Someone who knew how to drive could work in the motor pool, taking recruits to their work sites or hauling materials from one place to another in camp trucks. One enrollee who had learned to drive a truck before he joined the CCC was assigned to take an army supply truck down the winding mountain roads into town every day. He carried the letters the boys wrote to the post office to be mailed and picked up mail to be delivered to recruits. Then he stopped at the train station for supplies that had been shipped to camp. After that, he was off to a local creamery for the milk and butter the two hundred men in camp consumed each day. Last, he went to a bakery for huge trays of rolls and bread that would go onto dinner plates that night and into the hundreds of sandwiches the boys would eat for lunch the next day. He drove back up the mountain nearly floating in the aroma of fresh-baked bread.

Other young men who came to camp with skills often put them to use as well. When a company commander discovered that one of the boys in his charge had artistic talent, he assigned him to paint signs and posters for the camp.[63] Henry Rich knew a little about cooking and was soon a full-time cook at Camp Roosevelt, scrambling eggs or mashing potatoes for two hundred hungry boys in short order. He continued to work as a cook the whole time he was in the CCC.[64]

Another boy, Fred Helsley, was a member of a camp near Skyland. He had an unusual but important skill—he was very good at catching snakes. When the camp doctor asked for help catching a rattlesnake one day, Fred volunteered. He managed to catch two rattlers that afternoon. Over the next few weeks, Helsley caught copperheads and more rattlesnakes using a stick with a fork and a loop of string attached to it. Picture sneaking up on a poisonous rattlesnake with nothing but a stick and a fork for protection![65] But Fred wasn't afraid, and that was a good thing. With thousands of recruits working in forests and parks, snakebites were serious business.

The camp doctor sent the snakes Fred caught to the Forest Service, where they went to a laboratory to be "milked." The venom was used to make the antivenom that could save the life of someone bitten by the same kind of snake.[66] Fred spent a lot of time catching snakes. He was the only recruit in camp with the nerve to do the job. Even so, there wasn't always a supply of antivenom available, especially if a recruit was bitten at a far-off worksite.

As Shenandoah National Park recruit Ed Scott described that kind of incident,

> We was coming out of the mountain one evening, and it was raining . . . we was running through this orchard. And a rattlesnake hit [this boy] right on between the knee and the ankle, and tore up the skin . . . I stopped him and he laid down . . . I'd taken first aid training . . . and I give him a small operation right there. With a razor blade. I cut six

slices this-a-way and six this way, and . . . I put my
tourniquet on . . . I sucked all the blood out of it
that I could. And after a while, it was maybe for
fifteen or twenty minutes, I worked on him, sucking
the blood. Then we came out . . . And we'd taken
him in to sick bay, and the doctor . . . said you've
done all that I could do. So the boy laid around
there for a couple of weeks and his leg swelled up,
but he made it okay.[67]

As that first summer went on, recruits like Ed Scott, as well as
Woody, Henry, and thousands of others, saw trees growing taller
and roads growing longer and gained a sense of responsibility for
the jobs they were doing. They also learned to look out for their
camp mates when they worked on steep hillsides or used dangerous tools. And most of them realized they could trust those camp
mates to look out for them no matter where they were from or
what accent they had.

So far, the Civilian Conservation Corps was a success.

FDR enjoys lunch with CCC workers.

CHAPTER 7

Winning Support

The large number of tasks in progress at Shenandoah National Park was typical of the work done in most parks. But as many different kinds of jobs as there were in the Blue Ridge, Franklin Roosevelt pictured his Corps doing even more. He wanted camps in every state, and he wanted the boys doing every kind of conservation work that needed doing, not only park construction.

The young men could improve and protect the marshlands of Florida. They could build dams to control flooding in Tennessee. Crews could rid the swamps of North Carolina and Delaware of disease-carrying mosquitoes and construct lodges and campgrounds in the parks of Arizona and California. And what about the damage that had been done to the nation's forests and the constant threat of forest fires all over the country? The Corps could replant the woods and build fire roads and watchtowers that would be a great help. And of course, the terrible environmental destruction of the Dust Bowl had to be dealt with. Soil experts would need a lot of manpower to turn that disaster around. Perhaps FDR should have asked for a million or two million boys instead of five hundred thousand.

The president seemed to have endless ideas for how the Corps could save natural and human resources and wanted to keep expanding the program. But his ideas could move forward only if Congress provided more money and authorized the CCC for the next year and the next. Roosevelt knew the boys already at work were the key to getting that support.

One morning in mid-August, 1933, the recruits at Skyland heard an announcement they could hardly believe. President Franklin Roosevelt was coming to visit. The boys at the first CCC camps in Shenandoah National Park got busy. They made up their bunks and tidied their camps every morning just as recruits at all the CCC camps across the country did. Cleaning a barracks or camp is called *policing*, and anyone who didn't do his chores and keep his barracks space shipshape was soon peeling potatoes or scrubbing latrines. But on this warm August day, the boys at the Shenandoah camps really scrambled to make everything shine.

The president intended to visit the Shenandoah camps to see the park's progress and find out firsthand how the boys were doing. His interest was real. But he also hoped his visit would persuade still-hesitant people in Washington and elsewhere that his favorite program should go forward after the first year with more and more young men and projects.

Roosevelt rode in the backseat of a sleek, open car under

blue skies. He liked driving or riding in convertibles with the top down—the wind and air gave him a sense of physical freedom. From the backseat of a convertible, the president could connect with Americans in his "happy way of waving and smiling"[68] that made people feel like he was a friend. He often asked his driver to stop when he saw people along the way. Imagine going outside to do yard work and having the president of the United States stop to chat. FDR liked to talk to people from his car. The leg braces didn't matter when he was sitting in a convertible, and no one had to see him being lifted in or out. This day was no different, and FDR was in a very good mood as the car made its way along the winding mountain road in the early morning sun.

Just a few months into the project, Skyline Drive and the rest of the park were a long way from being finished, but Roosevelt was pleased with the progress he saw that August day. The stone walls looked wonderful and most of the ghost trees were gone. Good reports had come in from CCC projects all over the country, but seeing some of the work in person was a real treat.

Roosevelt had hoped to recruit 250,000 young men by July 4. In fact, Frances Perkins and the Department of Labor had enrolled over 275,000 recruits in 1,300 camps by Independence Day.[69] More young men lined up to join the CCC every day. But as popular as the Corps had become in its first few months, opposition persisted.

In the early days of the CCC, a number of Americans who liked the idea of a Civilian Conservation Corps objected to having

Hispanics in the CCC

Hispanic enrollees in the CCC were not officially segregated from whites the way African Americans were, but they still experienced discrimination. Most Hispanic recruits came from the southwestern United States and were of Mexican ancestry. Often they were assigned to Hispanic-majority companies in isolated areas. One such camp was at Big Bend National Park in West Texas. The park is largely a desert area filled with volcanic rock formations. Daily summer temperatures average over 100 degrees and sometimes reach 120 degrees. The CCC company that worked in the park building mountain roads and hiking trails was over 80 percent Hispanic. They worked year-round, even in the worst heat of the summer, using shovels and blasting equipment to move thousands of tons of dirt and  rock. The early recruits lived in tents rather than barracks, and the nearest town was eighty-five miles away. The men knew that even if they could get to town, they were likely to be turned away at restaurants or told to go "back" to Mexico, a place they had never lived. Their experience was typical of other Hispanic-majority companies. Even so, thousands of Hispanic young men joined the CCC and learned skills that led to future jobs.

a camp near where they lived. Part of their concern came from long years of prejudice. Whites in much of the nation did not want black recruits working near them, and in the Southwest, business owners often refused to serve Mexican American recruits when they came into town. And just like the boys themselves, they were afraid that young men from other parts of the country who looked different or came from immigrant families and spoke with foreign accents would cause problems. Most camps, of course, were planned for rural areas, and many people in those regions assumed that any recruit from a city breadline was probably a troublemaker, a bum, riffraff. No one wanted hooligans close by. And almost everyone worried about how two hundred energetic young men would behave in a small town on a Saturday night. As one Marylander described it,

> When some of the local residents found out that
> their community was being "invaded" by all these
> young men, they became quite perturbed. They
> feared that their property would be stolen by
> these outsiders and their women and daughters
> violated.[70]

The CCC might be a good idea, these people thought, but it would be better if the camps were near someone else's town.

Roosevelt was confident that boys like Woody Wilson—hardworking, honest, and polite—could win over people who had concerns about the CCC. That was why he was happy to have two or three carloads of reporters and cameramen follow him to Shenandoah National Park for his visit. They'd put pictures and stories of his trip in newspapers and on movie theater newsreels everywhere—exactly what he wanted. He also invited some important guests to come along.

Interior Secretary Harold Ickes and Agriculture Secretary Henry Wallace were with FDR that day. They needed to see the camps as much as the president did. And Roosevelt had also invited a man named William Green. He wanted Green to see for himself what the Civilian Conservation Corps was all about.

William Green was the head of the American Federation of Labor, an organization of many labor unions. He had opposed the CCC from the start. For one thing, he worried that regular employers would try to copy the CCC's one-dollar-a-day salary no matter how much Frances Perkins argued before Congress that that wouldn't happen. And despite Secretary Dern's promises, Green worried that with the military running the camps, the boys would soon be just like soldiers.[71] He agreed with the majority of Americans in the 1930s that the United States Army should be quite small in peacetime.

The AFL existed to represent workers. Part of William Green's job as head of the AFL was to make sure Congress understood the problems workers faced. Green was good at his job and often reminded congressmen that union workers voted by the thousands. Those congressmen listened carefully to what William

What's a Labor Union?

Labor unions are organizations of workers who join together to push for good wages, safe working conditions, and more. Unions were formed in the United States during the mid-1800s as industry changed. Employers and employees in new and much bigger factories, mills, and mines did not know one another personally. A single worker asking for higher wages or safer working conditions would be fired, and someone else would take his place. But when workers came together in unions, they had power. At first many people feared that unions would try to overthrow the government or take over industry. Over time, those fears faded and both the public and the government recognized workers' right to organize. By the 1930s, unions had won many victories for workers, including a workday of eight hours instead of twelve, a five-day work week instead of six, an end to child labor, and the beginnings of government safety regulations.

Green had to say about issues involving labor. FDR, therefore, needed Green on his side when it came to the CCC. He had tried to win him over by appointing a union leader, Robert Fechner, as director of the Corps. But even months in, Green wasn't happy with the idea of the CCC. Now Roosevelt was counting on Woody and all the others to change Green's mind for him.

As the presidential caravan of cars got to the first of the Shenandoah camps in operation in August, the recruits stood at attention like soldiers ready for inspection. There were no salutes or drills, though. As Roosevelt had said, this wasn't the military. The moment they got the signal, the boys broke formation and crowded around the president's car, cheering and jostling to shake hands with the man who had changed their lives.

At Big Meadows, Roosevelt sat at the head of a long plank table on the edge of the field that gave the camp its name, the field where Native American peoples had spent summers thousands of years earlier. Out came platters of steak with mounds of mashed potatoes, green beans, salad, and rolls, followed by fresh apple pie for dessert.[72] It looked like a real feast and this was a special occasion, but the food was typical of what the boys had for dinner regularly. The guests breathed in the sweet, clean air. Around them, birds sang, bees hummed. It was hard to imagine a nicer scene.

The president ate with enthusiasm and then spoke to the young men around him. "It's very good to be here at these

Virginia Civilian Conservation Corps camps," he said as the cameras rolled.

> I wish I could see them all over the country. I
> hope . . . they are in as fine condition as the camps
> that I've seen today. I wish that I could take a
> couple of months off from the White House and
> come down here and live with them, because I
> know I'd get full of health the way they have.[73]

Roosevelt was right that the boys had gotten "full of health." Recruits stood straight now with muscles showing beneath their shirts—muscles that could carry a hundred pounds of telephone cable up a mountainside. Coughs and runny noses had cleared up. They had gained weight, too.

Seventy-five percent of recruits were underweight when they enrolled. Some were weak with hunger and malnutrition.[74] FDR joked that while he was trying to lose twelve pounds, these boys were gaining that much in their first weeks in camp. It was true. Most enrollees did gain a needed ten or twelve pounds in just a few weeks.

Recruit Bill Stangl had never even seen a pancake or a grapefruit before joining the Corps. "All I had in my life before I came to the CCC was a cup of coffee and a piece of bread," he said, describing mornings at home.[75] The pancakes he could figure out, but he needed help learning how to eat a grapefruit.

An ordinary breakfast at camp included oatmeal, bacon, eggs, bread and butter, fruit, and all the milk a fellow wanted. At dinner, recruits who had been skipping meals to let their brothers and sisters eat dug into feasts like the one the president had just had. They couldn't seem to get enough.

Camp cooks requested bigger food budgets and more army surplus supplies to meet the demand for "unheard of quantities of food."[76] Bakers, butchers, and grocers in towns near the camps sold more goods than they had in several years. Roosevelt's Tree Army was building more than a park—it was building local economies, too.

The president finished his visit at Big Meadows and then continued another ten miles up Skyline Drive to the Skyland camp for a quick inspection. He and the others saw tidy rows of tents and a massive flagpole made from a tree trunk. The mess hall and kitchen building, as well as a shower and toilet building, were nearly finished. The visitors spent only a few minutes with the boys and were on their way again. The Front Royal camp, which had opened in June, was at the northern end of the park and a forty-mile drive from Skyland.

As brief as Roosevelt's visit was, Woody Wilson never forgot it. Neither did his camp mates. They had joined the CCC feeling like helpless, hopeless failures. Now the president of the United States had come to say he was proud of them.

Roosevelt had reason to be proud. The CCC boys in the Shenandoah camps provided living proof that his conservation employment plan was working for both the environment and the young men. Just as important to Roosevelt, those boys might one day teach their children about conservation. And the president wouldn't mind a bit if they decided to vote for Democrats for the rest of their lives.

FDR's strategy paid off. The film of his visit played as a newsreel in movie theaters from one side of the country to the other, and photographs appeared in newspapers and magazines. Letters asking for camps were already flooding the White House and Congress. Now, even people who had been fearful of the Corps wrote to encourage their representatives in Congress to support the CCC and bring camps to sites near their towns. And AFL leader William Green sent the president a note saying his visit to the Blue Ridge was "one of the most pleasing experiences" he'd ever had. He now "could not help but view the whole project in a most sympathetic way."[77] Congress was very likely to continue appropriating money for the CCC.

Strong public support and funding from Congress meant that more and more men could join the Civilian Conservation Corps. Already, the Corps had enrolled twelve thousand Native Americans who lived on reservations—some of the poorest places in the country. The CCC's Indian Division was run separately from the larger CCC and operated at the tribal level, allowing individual reservations to organize men and projects in a way that best suited their needs. Native Americans could join the

CCC without age limits, marriage restrictions, or a set six-month enrollment period.[78] They would work near their homes making badly needed improvements to the reservations, including new school buildings and sewage treatment plants. They would also restore millions of acres of farming and grazing land. No president had ever done as much to promote the economies of the nation's American Indian peoples.[79]

Like the Indian recruits, unemployed World War I veterans were invited to join without age limits or marriage restrictions. These veterans weren't young boys—they'd been to war, and most had families. Grateful for the possibility of work, they enrolled by the thousands, many of them dressed in worn suits and ties. Climbing off buses and trucks, they literally ran to get in recruitment lines before the opportunity was gone.

The CCC also changed its minimum age for regular recruits from eighteen to seventeen. Enrollees continued to sign up for six-month stints, but now they could reenlist after their first six months and serve up to two years in the Corps. Thousands of young men cheered that news. They were eager to stay with the Civilian Conservation Corps, and the CCC was glad to have them. Recruits who had gained strength and experience could be models for new enrollees and fill some leadership positions. Even so, new boys just off the breadlines needed professionals to teach them the specific skills their work demanded. The answer was Local Experienced Men, or LEMs.

The Corps hired some 35,000 unemployed men who lived

near a CCC camp and had experience in the kinds of work the recruits in the camp near them were doing. The LEMs would teach the boys what they needed to know.

Some LEMs had cut timber all their lives. They showed enrollees how to handle an ax and a two-man saw safely and effectively. Others had worked in road or housing construction before the Depression destroyed those jobs. They knew how to absorb the vibrations of a jackhammer or hammer a thousand nails without breaking any fingers or getting infections from bad blisters. They taught recruits how to measure wood correctly and cut angles and joints.

The local men had done all sorts of skilled jobs, but like many other workers, they'd been unemployed for two or three years. The small salary the CCC paid them helped support their families and the communities where they spent the money on food and other necessities. In return, many LEMs did far more than teach the boys work skills. They became father figures to recruits who didn't have fathers at home. They helped boys get past their homesickness, and they showed them how to apply the skills they were learning to new tasks and perhaps future jobs.

The CCC was offering opportunities to far more men than the boys on city breadlines Roosevelt had first mentioned, and Americans approved. But one issue remained a problem—racial prejudice and discrimination.

Representative Oscar De Priest's amendment to the Emergency Conservation Work Act had opened the Corps to African

Americans, but an amendment to one piece of legislation couldn't change the way most Americans thought. The fact was that racism, discrimination, and segregation were part of daily life in the United States—by custom in the North, and by law in the South.

Frances Perkins at the Department of Labor was furious when she learned that white Civilian Conservation Corp recruiters in the South weren't advertising the CCC to African Americans and were finding excuses to turn young black men away if they did try to join. Perkins believed in equality. One of the first things she had insisted on as secretary of labor was the integration of the cafeteria at the department's headquarters building, a policy that upset a lot of people in 1933.[80] Perkins couldn't oversee every local volunteer recruiter in the country to be sure they followed the rules, but the man she had hired as director of CCC hiring warned that the CCC would hire no young men at all if recruiters refused to accept blacks who applied.[81] Slowly, more blacks were enrolled.

The camps themselves were another issue.

Most recruits who had a hard time living with young men who sounded or looked a bit different eventually accepted one another. But some flatly refused to share barracks with men of another race. And a lot of camp officers who didn't want blacks in their companies ignored the law and let those young men—men like Houston Pritchett—know they weren't welcome. Pritchett had assumed when he joined the CCC that he would face prejudice. Racism was so much a part of his life, he said, that he expected discrimination in everything he did.[82] But the Civilian Conservation Corps should have been different—Congress had said so. Sadly, in many ways, it wasn't.

Frances Perkins was disappointed and angry that so many camp commanders expressed such racism. But there was little she could do about it. The army was completely segregated at the time (President Harry Truman ordered the military to integrate in 1947), and many of the reserve officers hired to run CCC camps were convinced that segregation was right for the army and right for the Corps.

CCC Director Robert Fechner had grown up in the South in a time when few white people in that part of the country questioned racism. In 1935 he decided to avoid conflict with white camp officers and recruits by ordering that all enrollees be segregated into white companies and black companies.[83] That was a blow to the men at integrated camps where everything was going well. As one white recruit said of Camp Herod in Illinois, the black enrollees there were "a fine bunch of men" and they had no race-related problems. He was very sorry to hear that the CCC was going to "de-integrate."[84] And in Washington State, a CCC company of men from Massachusetts telegrammed Director Fechner to protest the segregation policy. Six of the nearly two hundred men in the company were African Americans, and no one wanted the company broken up.[85]

Fechner didn't see the order he'd given as discrimination. How could that be? He believed he was following "the spirit and letter" of the law and didn't think segregation *was* discrimination. After all, he said, enrollees at every camp had the "same types of work, have identical equipment, are served the same food, and have the same quarters."[86] The camps were separate but equal.

Like Perkins, interior secretary Harold Ickes was outraged at Fechner's decision to segregate the CCC. Ickes despised segregation. He was a white lawyer who had championed civil rights for years, but without an order from Roosevelt himself, there was little Ickes or Perkins or anyone else could do about the situation. Unfortunately, neither Ickes nor Perkins was able to convince the president to issue that order.

Director Fechner may have intended to solve a problem by segregating the camps, but having all-white and all-black camps created another problem. Fechner described it when he said, "There is hardly a locality in this country that looks favorably, or even with indifference, on the location of a Negro CCC camp in their vicinity."[87] In other words, white communities didn't want black CCC camps near them. So Fechner decided to assign most African American companies to camps in very remote areas, far from neighboring towns. Of course, that left those young men in isolated areas and often in harsh climates, with few opportunities for recreation outside of camp. Was that equal? The director said it was, and Roosevelt didn't overrule him.

It was clear that Oscar De Priest's amendment was not going to accomplish all he'd hoped for. But it did have a positive, if limited, effect on the Corps. About 10 percent of Corps enrollees

Separate but Equal

For decades, many government officials and business owners claimed that segregation in schools, the military, workplaces, public parks, and the like was *not* discrimination. They defended the separation of whites and blacks based on an 1896 Supreme Court decision. In the case of *Plessy v. Ferguson*, the court had ruled that racial segregation is constitutional as long as both races are given  facilities that are equal. But in many parts of the South, there were no parks or decent neighborhoods for African Americans at all. There were no well-paying jobs, either, and in the neighborhoods where blacks were allowed to live, the streets were dirt and there were no sewers or streetlights. Blacks were often arrested for using white facilities or trying to vote. Things were better in the North, but blacks still suffered serious discrimination. Schools in the North and especially in the South were glaring examples of inequality.

In 1954 a new case about segregation came before the Supreme Court. In *Brown v. Board of Education*, attorney Thurgood Marshall argued that racially segregated schools can never be equal. Research showed that they harmed both African American and white children because they made black children feel inferior to whites and white children feel superior to blacks. That was partly because the buildings, playgrounds, bathrooms, desks, and books at schools for African American children were never equal in quality to those for whites. The court agreed with Marshall and ruled that segregated schools violated the Constitution and could not be allowed. Ten years later, Congress passed the Civil Rights Act of 1964, outlawing segregation and discrimination in most other public places.

were African Americans (African Americans made up 9.7 percent of the US population at the time). And despite the discrimination most of them experienced, they did learn job skills and were paid thirty dollars a month just like all the other recruits. In the 1930s, that was nearly unheard of. Moreover, many of the white reserve officers who were very reluctant to command African American companies changed their thinking as they saw that black enrollees were just as hardworking, capable, and patriotic as white enrollees. Getting to know people they'd been taught to fear made all the difference. That was a valuable lesson.

Before the end of 1933, young men of every race and background had joined the Corps, usually for the promise of work and food. Even those in the most isolated camps had plenty of both. And enrollees were finding that there was much more to the CCC than a job and three meals a day.

CHAPTER 8

More Than Work

When President Roosevelt saw the boys of Company 334 at Skyland, they were so used to their daily routine that they hardly needed the call of a bugle to get them up and moving in the morning. They'd learned to follow the rules and take care of chores without reminders, too, so they wouldn't lose their free time.

Bedbugs were everybody's job. The tiny brown insects, so small they're hard to see, feed on human blood. Their bites cause itching and sometimes a rash, and no one sharing a bed with them gets a good night's sleep. "We put a, a kind of mixture of turpentine and some sort of chemical [on the floors] to kill those darn things," one recruit said. "After about two weeks, they'd start coming back . . . we'd scrub them barracks floors as much as we could."[88] The battle never ended. Neither did the itching.

Some boys spent time and elbow grease making the stainless-steel sinks in the bathhouses shine, while others got stuck with latrine-cleaning duty. The mess halls were kept spotless too, and someone had to pull the weeds around the flagpole.

Bedbugs mattered, of course, and everyone agreed clean toilets were a good idea. But who really cared if the sinks sparkled or the weeds were pulled? Camp commanders did. Those military men ran their camps in military style. Spit and shine, spic and span. Part of the CCC's plan for the boys was that recruits would learn to take pride in giving every job their best effort, from planting trees to peeling potatoes.

There were plans for the boys' free time, too. Roosevelt wanted to offer opportunities in every CCC camp in the country, whether it was in the mountains of New Hampshire or at the bottom of the Grand Canyon, for the recruits to play and learn when they were not working.

During the three hours between dinner and lights out, and most of Saturday and Sunday, the recruits had almost no responsibilities—just free time. Picture that. Now take away the Internet, computers, electronic games, televisions, and phones. How did the boys fill all those free hours? For them, the possibilities were endless.

Henry Rich was a natural musician, the kind of fellow who could pick up an instrument and teach himself to play in no time. In the evenings, he played the old guitar he'd brought with him to Camp Roosevelt, and before long he joined a group called the Harmonica and String Sextet. When he wasn't ladling stew from a huge pot, or turning gallons of batter into pancakes, he and the other five members of the group practiced and performed hymns, old-time songs, and the mountain music that came from the hills of Appalachia, where the CCC was building the Blue Ridge Parkway. Many recruits from Virginia, West Virginia, Tennessee, and the Carolinas had grown up with the sound. Bands formed at most camps, some with a dozen members playing everything from accordions and banjos to washboards and zithers. Those who didn't play listened, clapped, and tapped their feet while the musicians' fingers flew. Some recruits clogged well enough to put on their own dance shows.

Woody was a big fan of the camp bands. He didn't play an instrument, but he admired anyone who could and liked to see them perform as he had when he lived close enough to Washington, DC, to go into the city now and then for the music. He liked fishing and swimming, too. Not many people had pools to go to in those days. They went to lakes, ponds, or rivers to swim. So the men looked for the natural pools that formed below waterfalls or swam in ponds near their camps until the fall weather chased them out. There were plenty of other activities as well.

Recruits at Big Meadows built a baseball diamond as good as any in most towns. They formed a team that played against the Skyland and Camp Roosevelt teams. That led to a league, and most teams raised money for major-league-style uniforms. On Sunday evenings truckloads of recruits followed their camp's team to cheer them on against other camps. They played against local town teams and teams from nearby colleges, too. Tournament trophies went on display in camp recreation halls. That kind of thing boosted morale for the whole company.

Mountain Music

The people of the Appalachian Mountains have been playing mountain music since their Irish, Scottish, and English ancestors settled the region in the 1600s. Songs were handed down from one generation to the next, and children learned to dance and play instruments very early. The invention of the phonograph in the late 1800s, and the popularity of radio by the 1920s, brought mountain music to the people across the country. Recordings and radio also spread jazz—originally from New Orleans—nationwide. When mountain music performers began to adopt some jazz traits, a new genre called bluegrass music was born. Bluegrass is still played today, but it is also the origin of another, very popular kind of music: country.

Baseball wasn't the only popular sport. The men played football and basketball. They had wrestling and boxing matches and formed track teams. And for some enrollees, sports were more than fun. They opened doors to a better future.

Tyree Grydon grew up in the Shenandoah Valley and worked in the CCC at Shenandoah National Park. He was a quick, wiry young man who played a lot of sports but really excelled at track, even breaking a record in a meet against college men at Virginia Tech. As he liked to describe it with a laugh, "I won a gold medal in the 440. They wanted me to break the world record, but I said no."[89]

Scouts from the University of Richmond saw Tyree run and offered him an athletic scholarship. The same thing happened with the Corps' athletes in other parts of the country. Some of those young men went from the streets to a CCC barracks and then to a college dorm, something they had never dreamed was possible.

Other recruits got a chance for an education right in their own camps. President Roosevelt knew that thousands of CCC enrollees came to camp not knowing how to read or write. Think of being as old as seventeen or eighteen and unable to read a street sign or put a signature on a piece of paper. Roosevelt wanted to make sure that none of those boys would leave the Corps illiterate. He appointed a director of education and hired more than a thousand out-of-work teachers to oversee education programs at the camps. Local volunteer teachers and camp officers were soon instructing young men who'd never been to school.

Not every boy who needed those classes took advantage of them. The last thing a lot of recruits wanted to do after a long day of hard work was go to school. Many were ashamed to admit they couldn't read. Others didn't see much point in learning academic skills when they were likely to be construction workers or fishermen or farmers for the rest of their lives. And some camp commanders wouldn't encourage the boys to sign up because they saw the programs as frills or extras and not terribly important. Still, at least forty thousand CCC recruits learned to read and write in the Corps.

Boys like Woody who had finished only the eighth grade could take high school classes or correspondence courses—somewhat like the online courses of today but completed by mail. Thousands finished their high school equivalency or General Educational Development (GED) test, which helped them find jobs after they left the Corps. Others took college courses by correspondence.

Volunteer instructors and enrollees who had skills or knowledge to share offered classes in art, music, first aid, mechanics, carpentry, welding, forestry, photography, typing, and more. One of the most popular classes was amateur (or ham) radio. Recruits learned to operate the two-way radios and could contact other ham radio operators hundreds of miles away. Many of the boys had never had a telephone at home, and communicating with someone from any distance was a new experience.

Every camp had its own newspaper, too, written and published by men taking journalism classes. The papers reported on camp news and announcements, let the enrollees know about events in town and around the country, and often had cartoons drawn by recruits as well as essays and poetry written by the young men themselves. The boys could also spend their free time in the camp recreation hall, where they might play cards or read one of the hundreds of donated books in the camp library.

A CCC recruit could stay busy without ever leaving camp. But seeing the same faces every day—all of them male—made most of the young men itchy to go into whatever town was fairly close. Often, that wasn't easy for black or Latino enrollees, but for white recruits and minorities in some places, a little money in their pockets was all they needed. They received only five dollars of their pay each month, since the rest went to their families, but a lot of boys found ways to earn extra spending money on the side.

Some young men cut other recruits' hair for a few pennies. Some offered guitar or banjo lessons. A fellow without any special skills might do laundry or iron shirts for pay. And when winter came, recruits were happy to chip in for someone to keep the barrack's woodstove burning.

Fifty cents could get an enrollee a movie, a bag of popcorn, and an ice cream sundae afterward on a Saturday afternoon. Some towns had roller-skating rinks where admission was about thirty-five cents for the evening, or bowling alleys that charged twenty cents a game. And most places had a restaurant or two where a hot dog or barbecue sandwich might cost twenty cents and spaghetti and meatballs forty cents.

Then there were dances. Many camps hosted community dances in their recreation halls. The men made sure they had clean nails, pressed shirts, and carefully combed hair on those nights. They might add a dab of aftershave, too. Some even took dancing lessons from their pals before the big day. Towns also held socials, as they called them, on Saturday nights or at least on special occasions, and most boys were happy to get dressed as nicely as they could and go to a local dance.

"There might be twenty-five or thirty of us in the back of a truck," Frank Davis, a recruit in North Carolina, said. "We would sing songs as we rode down the mountain. . . . I can still hear that truckload of boys stomping their feet and singing."[90]

Local bands played mountain dance music or big band favorites. Local girls wore their nicest dresses, even if they were borrowed or made from the remnants of hand-me-downs. They curled their hair and tried to look their best.

Frank Davis admitted,

> I had never been to a dance and never danced with
> a girl. . . . A dance was coming up and we made an
> agreement that if we didn't dance with a girl that
> night we would have to run through a belt line the
> next day . . . a double line of boys with their belts in
> their hands who would take a whack at you as you
> ran through.[91]

Frank did ask a girl to dance that night, but as they were moving to a slow number, his face close to the top of her head, the gum he was chewing got stuck in her hair without her realizing it. He kept dancing as if everything was fine, but when they stopped, he opened his mouth to let the gum out, backed away, and ran. It was quite a while before he got up the nerve to attend another dance.[92]

Fortunately, not many boys had to run from their dance partners. Occasionally, those dances even led to a serious romance between a young man from a CCC camp and a young woman from a local town.

Most CCC boys liked their work and were happy to spend their free time taking classes or enjoying some recreation. But a small number of enrollees couldn't seem to adjust to life in the Corps. Overall, about 8 percent of recruits around the country left in the early days of their enlistments. A few who stayed might have been better off leaving. They weren't ready to follow rules, work hard, and accept responsibility. Instead they did the very things that local communities feared they might do.

The CCC gave the men instructions and rules for their behavior, not just at camp and on the job, but during their free time as well. The men's good behavior was important to the Corps' success. If recruits made a bad impression on communities, President Roosevelt's Tree Army could lose support and fall apart. So when a recruit was caught violating the rules, he could expect to lose any chance of leaving camp and faced the possibility of being thrown out of the Corps. But it wasn't just community relations that made discipline a serious concern. Good behavior was important to the men's health and safety. The dangers of bad behavior were very real.

One beautiful Sunday afternoon in Tennessee, a recruit with a reputation for trouble got hold of some moonshine. It wasn't the first time. But on this warm spring day the liquor took effect quickly. Drunk, the boy made a terrible decision. He decided to jump from a bridge into a rain-swollen river. His friends saw what he was about to do but couldn't stop him. They watched in horror as he disappeared into the swirling brown water. One young man raced along the river bank, frantically trying to reach his camp mate. He couldn't. For weeks after he thought about what had happened and where the river had taken the boy. Eventually, the recruit's body was found in a tangled mass of weeds.

An Ohio recruit made a similar, tragic mistake with water. He didn't think to check the water's depth and dove into shallow water, breaking his neck and dying instantly.[93] The shock for all the other boys in his camp was terrible, especially because his death could have been easily avoided.

Alcohol was often to blame for the young men's mishaps. They were told not to drink when they went to town, and camp officers tried to explain the dangers of drinking. It didn't always work. In one case, some friends went into town on a Saturday night and broke the rules. On the way back to camp, their car hit a bus and one enrollee was thrown into a telephone pole. There was nothing anyone could do. He died on the spot. Just as those boys had begun to have hope for the future, they threw it away. Senseless deaths like those pulled whole companies down.[94]

Fortunately, that kind of tragedy was rare. Much more often, people who had worried about having hundreds of young men close to their small towns came to love the CCC. They got to know recruits who shopped at their stores or ate at their restaurants and found they were just like their own sons, even if they did look and sound a bit different. And of course, they appreciated the enrollees' business, since every little bit of money the boys spent in town helped. In some places, business owners even pitched in to buy uniforms for the nearby camp's baseball team.[95] And recruits who attended churches in town frequently got invitations to Sunday supper at families' homes.

Contacts between CCC recruits and townspeople did more than boost support for the Corps. They had a long-lasting impact on Americans' opinions of people from parts of the country they'd never visited. Little by little, the Civilian Conservation Corps was changing attitudes as well as landscapes.

CCC workers on their way to fight a forest fire.

CHAPTER 9

Across the Country

Brand-new parks like Shenandoah in Virginia and Great Smoky Mountains in North Carolina and Tennessee changed landscapes in the eastern United States. In the West, while some CCC companies built new parks, more worked to repair and improve existing national parks in some of the country's most amazing and challenging places.

Grand Canyon National Park in Arizona, for example, is the site of one of the world's great natural wonders. The canyon, formed over millions of years by the rushing water of the Colorado River, is nearly three hundred miles long, one mile deep, and layered with impossibly beautiful colors. Ancient Pueblo peoples believed the canyon to be a holy place, and most visitors today still find seeing it a spiritual experience.

Imagine being a young recruit from the flat, open plains of Texas assigned to Company 818 of the Civilian Conservation Corps. Where was the company's camp? In winter, it was at the bottom of the Grand Canyon. There are no roads into the floor of the canyon even today. The only ways to reach the bottom of the canyon in the park are by hiking down at least nine miles of steep trails, riding on the back of a mule down those trails, or rafting in through the rapids of the Colorado River.

The boys of Company 818 reached their camp on foot. Their supplies arrived daily on the backs of mules, whose surefooted confidence on the narrow zigzag paths was (and still is) legendary. Once the mules' packs were unloaded, the animals spent the night in the canyon and then carried trash out the next day.

Recruits were in the park to improve the existing trails used by hikers and mules, and to build new trails. Winter was the best time for that kind of work because temperatures in the bottom of the canyon were mild, with little threat of the snow and ice that shut down the North Rim of the canyon for several months each year.

Good weather was important as Company 818 took on the challenge of constructing the Colorado River Trail—the most difficult trail ever built at the Grand Canyon. Even in perfect weather, it took courage to stand on a ledge just a foot wide with a wall of rock going up one side and a drop of several hundred feet on the other. But the men did it, though they might have been jealous of those mules with their calm nature and four sure feet. Slowly, using picks, jackhammers, and some blasting, the enrollees carved out the remarkable trail that hikers still use today. But not everyone could handle the nerve-racking labor.

Recruits from Arizona were familiar with the craggy cliffs of canyons and mountains. But those from Oklahoma and Texas had grown up surrounded by miles of wide-open flat spaces. Sometimes those young men couldn't bring themselves to balance on a narrow ledge and swing a pick. They had to be assigned to other kinds of work. As one Arizona man said of his camp, "You are surrounded by mountains and you don't really see out. Those boys from Texas were used to the wide-open plains, and I suppose just couldn't take it there."[96]

In summer, when the temperature deep in the canyon could reach 120 degrees, the men of Company 818 worked on the trails and buildings at the canyon's North Rim, some seven thousand feet above the base. There they breathed crisp, clean air filled with the scent of ponderosa pine and Douglas fir. Even in July, early morning temperatures could be in the forties. But not everyone liked the North Rim camp. Similar to the winter camp, it was incredibly remote. There were no towns to go to on a Saturday night and no local girls to invite to a company dance. No movie theaters or restaurants or anything else. For all the canyon's wonder, that kind of isolation could wear a man down even if the park was worth the effort.[97]

Parks, of course, were only one part of President Roosevelt's vision for the CCC. Saving farmland was another. FDR asked Congress to create a Soil Erosion Service (soon called the Soil Conservation Service) and put a man named Hugh Bennett in charge. Bennett had spent nearly thirty years at the Department of Agriculture studying soil depletion, erosion, and conservation. For most of that time, he'd been trying to get Congress and the public to pay attention to what he'd learned, but it was an uphill battle.

Farmers, and even a small number of scientists, refused to believe that human activity—the way farmers farmed—had anything to do with the nation's farmland crisis. They insisted that weather alone had caused the problems on the Great Plains, and nothing could be done about it. The Dust Bowl was simply part of nature's cycle, they said. Bennett knew that wasn't true. He and another researcher wrote a paper called "Soil Erosion: A National Menace."[98] Finally, some congressmen noticed. They represented farmers in the Great Plains states who had fallen into poverty because of poor crops and drought. Could there really be a way to save the soil?

Now, as head of the new Soil Conservation Service, Bennett could put his ideas to work. He hired soil experts—many of them from land-grant universities—to set up demonstration areas around the country. In each area, the experts would figure out the best ways to improve the soil and prevent future erosion and flooding in that particular area. CCC recruits would help demonstrate those methods, building earthen dams and fences, terracing hillsides, planting seedlings in contour (curved) rows, and more.

Eventually, CCC enrollees worked in almost every state, with over 450 soil conservation areas nationwide. Farmers received information and lessons on the farming techniques that would be most efficient for them. The Corps assisted them in using the techniques.[99] Soon those farmers began to see the difference the changes made as the combination of scientific study and strong government support began a turnaround of the nation's farm-land.[100]

In the dry areas of the West, the young men of the CCC repaired aging, neglected irrigation systems. They built dams to create reservoirs for holding water. In wetter parts of the country, they built dams to help prevent flooding. Those projects, like the park projects, were carefully designed ahead of time. But CCC recruits also found themselves doing things no one had expected them to do.

One year in the Ohio River Valley of Indiana, rain fell nearly every day for a month, causing the Ohio River and its tributaries to overflow their banks. Water rose until towns became islands and whole families climbed onto their rooftops, desperate for rescue.[101]

CCC enrollees in the area stopped their regular work and set up shelters for people whose homes had washed away. Other recruits took boats and heavy trucks to get stranded people off their roofs and save as much property as they could. Farther south in Kentucky, young men transported more than two hundred families and their farm animals to higher ground as the water edged toward them.[102] Some of those recruits had never seen a farm animal up close. Now they were carrying chickens and lambs in their arms.

In Connecticut it was a hurricane that gave CCC workers jobs they hadn't bargained for. The fierce storm destroyed whole communities, and recruits working on parks in the state were sent to help with relief efforts. For weeks, they worked long days searching for missing people, clearing roads of downed trees and debris, and helping power companies restore electricity. Over the next six months, forty CCC camps from all over New England had their men clearing fallen trees from forests where they would pose fire hazards once they dried out.[103]

A number of boys who joined the Corps in eastern cities had been sent to camps in Utah, where they were needed to build roads into remote areas and establish campgrounds in parks. They even worked to improve rodeo arenas, something they certainly couldn't have done in New York or Boston. But one winter, the weather turned worse than the oldest locals could remember and the boys of the CCC became heroes.

In southern Utah, heavy snow followed heavy snow. Foot upon foot of snow blowing and drifting across ranchland stranded a million sheep. The sheep couldn't get to the grass in their pastures because of the deep drifts, and as the snow kept coming, they faced starvation. Sheep ranchers couldn't help more than a handful of the animals and were about to lose everything. A call for help went out to the CCC.

During the next ten days, recruits worked night and day in forty-degrees-below-zero temperatures to get truckloads of feed to the trapped animals. They hauled huge sleds when the trucks couldn't move and quickly learned to walk in snowshoes. At times, the driving white snow combined with heavy white clouds and feet of snow on the ground to nearly blind the men. But they could hear the sheep bleating, and that kept them moving. In the end, the men of the CCC saved hundreds of thousands of animals and kept the ranchers in business. They also rescued families trapped in their houses without food or fuel for heat.[104] By the time it was over, the recruits were exhausted, but those days made for amazing tales when the boys left the Corps and went home.

The stories go on and on. Between 1933 and 1941, the Civilian Conservation Corps helped out in emergencies all over the United States in all sorts of disasters—blizzards, floods, tornadoes, hurricanes, even a shipwreck. They worked in deserts, on seashores and grasslands, near cities, and in the middle of nowhere. But Roosevelt's first environmental priority was trees, and half of all CCC camps were in the nation's forests.

Edwin Hill left his family's small farm in Georgia to join the CCC at seventeen. His mother had died that year, and Ed couldn't bear the emptiness he felt at home. Besides, his family needed money, and Ed figured the Corps was the answer. He was right.

Assigned to Camp Hard Labor Creek, just thirty miles from home, Hill spent months helping to clear a creek bed of heavy trees and brush that caused flooding. It was useful work—work that could save farms downstream from serious losses. But when Ed reenlisted, he asked to be assigned as far away from Georgia as possible. It wasn't that he didn't love his family or home. He did. But Ed Hill realized that the Civilian Conservation Corps offered him a chance to see places he'd only read about. As he described it, "I made the most of it."[105]

Ed got his wish and soon joined a group of recruits on a train bound for Vancouver, Washington, in the far northwest corner of the country. On the way, they crossed open grazing land stretching as far as the eye could see in every direction. They watched cowboys on horseback guarding cattle herds. Ed even caught sight of the deer and the antelope people sang about in "Home on the Range." As the train chugged through Montana and Oregon, snow-covered mountains towered four times the height of Georgia's Appalachians. And when the boys stepped onto station platforms for a break at the stops along the way, they inhaled air so cold it burned their lungs.

Finally Ed got to Camp Skamania in southern Washington State, and when the camp commander learned he had a license to drive trucks, he got his assignment. As a company driver, Ed took men to their worksites each morning, put out lunch for them at noon, and drove them back to camp late in the day. They were clearing paths for fire roads in the forest, while other men erected fire watchtowers deep in the woods.

Most forestry leaders at the time believed that all forest fires had to be put out as quickly as possible. The goal was to protect timber, animals, and rivers and streams. That was one reason for putting hundreds of CCC camps in and near the national forests. The fire roads they built would allow firefighters and trucks into the most remote woods, and the watchtowers overlooking millions of acres of trees meant that rangers and fire watchers could send an alert soon after a fire got started. When the men of the Corps weren't building roads and towers, they assisted forest rangers and local men in actually fighting fires. One recruit in Arizona worked as a carpenter but said he felt like he "fought a million forest fires."[106]

Nationwide, recruits cleared thousands of miles of fire road-beds. They strung telephone lines across the forests for quick communication. The young men dug up mounds of underbrush that could ignite easily and made paths called firebreaks to keep flames from spreading over large areas. The New York Times said, "CCC men [have] buckled down to the task of fire-proofing the forests."[107]

Of course, no forest can be truly fireproofed. And today, forestry experts understand that naturally-occurring or controlled fires are good for forests over time. But Ed Hill's supervisors in Washington didn't know all that.

Ed hadn't been at Camp Skamania very long before fires were springing up everywhere and destroying thousands of acres of forest. An early, hot, dry summer that year had made forest fires a bigger hazard than usual. He and the rest of his company, as well as other CCC companies and many men from nearby towns, stopped their regular jobs to join the firefighters in their dangerous, difficult, draining work.

The men camped as close to the burning forests as was safe, sleeping on the ground and washing in a small mountain stream. No amount of washing, though, got rid of the sooty smell they all carried, but they were usually too tired and hungry to care. Teams of cooks took shifts, making food around the clock so crews coming back to camp in the middle of the night would have hearty meals. Those men needed huge amounts of food to fuel the energy and stamina it took to fight a fire.

One day Ed drove to the fire line to pick up an exhausted crew and take them back to camp. The men heaved themselves into the truck bed and Ed started off. But they'd gone only a few yards when the wind shifted and the fire crowned—whooshing and crackling through the tops of the trees from one side of the road to the other. In an instant, there was no way out. Ed Hill and his truckload of men were in a tunnel of flame. Years later, he remembered that day.

> I had no choice but to drive through the tunnel
> of fire with my load of flame tamers. Sparks from
> the burning trees ignited the canvas on the truck
> bed. . . . We continued nonstop through the land
> of fire to safety.[108]

It's hard to imagine the fear those men must have felt as the roof of the truck burst into flames. Ed pressed on while the crew tried to put out the fire over their heads. They managed to get through the ordeal, every one of them aware of how lucky they were.

Not all the men fighting fires had such good fortune.

As the fire worsened over the next few days, Ed continued his job of transporting crews. Late one afternoon, he went to get a group of men who'd been on the mountain since dawn. The hot, tired, hungry, thirsty firefighters trudged out of the forest. Without warning, one of the crewmen collapsed. Ed described what happened next.

> We immediately put our first aid training to use . . .
> trying desperately to revive him. We took turns giving
> him artificial respiration until it became certain
> that all our efforts were futile, that he was, in fact,
> beyond help.[109]

The Oregon man, in his fifties, had had a heart attack, probably from the exertion of fighting the fire all day and inhaling too much smoke. He wasn't in the CCC, and Ed had never met him, but Hill had never seen anyone die, and the experience shook him. He'd never used his first aid training that way, either, and never thought he would.

When Ed was unable to help the older worker, he realized how much he missed his own father back in Georgia. He thought about how quickly a life can be gone. Other recruits thought about those things too, especially when they lost one of their own.

In all, forty-seven CCC recruits in their teens and twenties perished while on fire duty—some when trees fell on them, some in bad falls, some when they were overcome by smoke and flame. In the Shoshone National Forest in Wyoming, fifteen men died in one terrible night when sudden strong winds caused a fire to jump ahead of them in all directions. They looked for a path to safety, but flames surrounded them and there was no escape.

Recruits and firefighters searched for the men as soon as they could make their way into the burned areas. When they found them, they led the injured survivors to aid in the nearest fire camp and carried their dead and dying companions out of the forest. Then they started fighting the fire again.[110]

During dry seasons, forest fires were a major concern in the East as well as the West. In the fall of 1938, seven CCC boys, ages seventeen to nineteen, died fighting a fire in Cameron County, Pennsylvania. An investigation found no evidence that camp leaders or others were at fault, but some recruits insisted that those deaths could have been avoided if the men had had more training and more time to rest. They'd fought fires throughout the previous day and were already tired before picking up their shovels and axes that terrible morning.[111]

As terrifying and devastating as fires could be, however, they weren't the major cause of serious injuries or deaths in the CCC. Motor vehicle accidents were the single biggest killer of recruits. Alcohol sometimes played a part in those crashes, but more frequently, steep, winding mountain roads or slick mud and ice were to blame. At Camp Hicks in Illinois, three men were killed and five injured when their camp truck ran off the edge of a road and overturned.[112] Similar accidents happened elsewhere, though some men who might have been hurt or killed were very lucky.

CCC recruit Lloyd Tripp, at another Illinois camp, recalled trying to clear trees from a hillside. He and another man drove their bulldozers along the side of the embankment, pushing trees down. Tripp warned the other driver not to get too close to the edge of the hill, but a few minutes later he heard frantic yelling. When he turned, he was horrified to see the other bulldozer hanging over the side of the steep hill, with his friend still in it and near panic. If the man leaned forward to get out of the driver's seat, the massive machine tipped farther over the edge. When he leaned back, the dozer steadied itself, but he couldn't get out. Shouting encouragement while he turned his own dozer around, Tripp made his way back along the road and was able to hook his bulldozer to the one in danger and pull it to safety. "I've never seen a guy so scared in my life,"[113] he said later.

The Corps lost young men to illnesses, too—appendicitis and pneumonia more often than any other diseases. There were also on-the-job accidents as the men worked with saws and hauled rocks, though those injuries usually involved bad cuts, broken bones, and sometimes a lost finger, but weren't fatal.

Camp commanders kept careful records of accidents. In the CCC's first year, the numbers added up to 288 injuries for every one thousand recruits. That was an unacceptable number, and a new safety division was created for the Corps with the goal of reducing the accidents. Every camp got orders to organize a safety council and provide more training in how to handle tools and other equipment. Posters went up to remind enrollees of new safety rules and safe practices. One way to avoid accidents, the young men were told, was to use a tool *only* to do what that tool was designed to do. "A wrench is not a hammer, a pick is not a crowbar, an axe is not a wedge."[114]

The accident rate improved in 1934 and again in 1935. It kept improving through the Corps' last full year in 1941, when the rate dropped to 81 out of one thousand recruits injured or killed. That accident rate was better than the rate for young men *not* in the Civilian Conservation Corps.[115]

Losing a camp mate was always hard, and the men of the CCC carried the memory of their coworkers and friends with them long after they left the Corps. Fortunately, deaths were rare and at many camps the most serious injuries were the sprains and occasional broken bones that occurred when the recruits played football or baseball. The vast majority of enrollees left the Corps much healthier than when they joined.

The young men of the CCC did all sorts of jobs in all sorts of places. Some worked close to home, some crossed the country. Camps like Skyland and Big Meadows, where the Corps worked to turn tens of thousands of acres into a park, stayed open the entire nine years the CCC existed. Where projects were small, camps closed after a few months, and the company working at that camp moved to another location and another kind of work. Some stayed with the Corps for six months, while others reenlisted for the two years they were allowed. But sooner or later, every CCC recruit had to say good-bye and move on with his life.

CCC members planting a tree in Shenandoah National Forest.

CHAPTER 10

Moving On

Woody Wilson had chosen to reenlist at the end of his first six months. He enjoyed the work he was doing on Skyline Drive and felt good that the twenty-five dollars going to his parents back in Herndon every month kept food on their table. The grocer in Herndon probably felt good about that too.

Winter came early to the Shenandoah region that year, with snow falling in October at Skyland and Big Meadows. Before the official end of autumn, Woody and his camp mates found snow on their pillows some mornings, and their boots frozen to the tent floors. By December, bitter cold settled in and the winds blew hard enough one night to tear some tents apart. The boys were left in the open with the temperature near zero as they scrambled to cram themselves into the camp's cars and trucks.

Work went on throughout the winter unless the snow was too deep to get to the work sites. Cold weather didn't stop anyone from building shelters and picnic tables and the like. And ghost trees could still be cut down and hauled away. But of course, recruits couldn't work on planting trees or shrubs or digging plants up when the ground was frozen. And no one can pave a roadbed that's covered in snow, so the boys had more free time than they did the rest of year. That was true at all the camps where winters were cold.

Wildflowers finally pushed through the remnants of snow in the Blue Ridge Mountains as the earliest CCC recruits neared the end of a year's enlistment. New recruits came to replace those who left. Like the first enrollees, they quickly started gaining strength, skills, and self-confidence. Woody had to decide soon if he wanted to reenlist for a third six-month period. His supervisors had given him excellent work reports, making him eligible for a possible promotion to supervising the new recruits. That would mean a little more money and was certainly something to think about.

One day in early March, however, a car pulled into the Skyland camp. A young man named George Chapell got out and asked for Woody. George had married Woody's sister Agnes a few years earlier, and he and Woody liked each other and got along well. That was one reason George had driven out to Skyland from Herndon. He didn't want Woody getting bad news from a stranger or over the phone. Woody was needed at home. His father, Thomas Wilson, had died.

News of his father's death was hard for Woody to absorb. The rest of the news was even harder. Tom Wilson had taken his own life.[116] Woody Wilson was about to make use of all the growing up he had done in the CCC.

With no job for three years, Mr. Wilson couldn't provide for his family, and he couldn't handle the shame he felt because of it. Thousands of proud men around the country felt the same way. The Great Depression had destroyed more than the nation's economy. It had destroyed human beings. And since no one understood the disease of depression very well in those days, there wasn't much help available.

Woody's father didn't leave a note explaining what pushed him to suicide. But he had started drinking too much and talking too little. On March 6, 1934, after his sister arrived at the house for a visit and was talking with Woody's mother, he went out to the backyard shed and shot himself.[117]

The next few days were a blur of relatives and neighbors coming in and out, and then the funeral. Woody stayed with his mother through the hubbub until things settled down, but the questions weren't going to go away. Was there something he could have done? Some way to have stopped the tragedy? Should he have been at home instead of at Skyland? No. Woody's work with the CCC had helped keep his family fed for nearly a year. His parents had every right to be proud of the young man he was becoming.

Woody made a decision. Though he was doing very well in the CCC, he wouldn't ask for another six months with the Corps, even it meant a promotion. But he would finish the time he'd

Gender Roles Today

Most Americans today accept the idea of women having both a job and a family and have become more comfortable with men who stay home with young children. But society still has expectations about what boys and girls, and men and women, should and shouldn't do, feel, and like as males or as females. Women in the military or in engineering have to prove themselves over and over in ways men don't. And men who go into nursing or teaching elementary school often have to explain themselves or defend their masculinity. Young boys face similar pressures. Research shows that there are very few differences between male and female brains. But boys are often mocked for wanting to play with dolls or kitchen toys. They are told to "man up" if they cry easily or happen to like the color pink. And adults frequently expect and accept violent behavior in boys that they would not accept in girls.[156] These attitudes harm both boys and girls, and men and women, just as attitudes of the 1930s did. Then, the expectation that a "real man" supported his family financially caused men who had lost their jobs to feel like failures and even led to some suicides.

already signed on for. Then he would come home to be with his mother. His older brothers and sisters were nearby to look in on her for the time being, so Woody would keep the pledge he'd made when he joined the Civilian Conservation Corps.

On June 30, 1934, Woodrow Wilson served his last day in the CCC. He and over a hundred other men attended a discharge ceremony and then sat down to their last Corps dinner—turkey with all the trimmings. The meal looked like a Thanksgiving feast, and in fact, there was a lot to be thankful for.[118]

Woody was leaving the Corps with an honorable discharge and a certificate of merit "in recognition of his fidelity, loyalty, and service." More important than those documents were the skills, self-discipline, and confidence he had gained. The Depression was far from over, but Woody was sure that with a good recommendation from the Corps and a new, positive, and mature attitude, he could find work at home. He was ready to meet whatever responsibilities lay ahead.

Woody moved back home with his mother and started job hunting. He soon found work delivering the blocks of ice that kept kitchen iceboxes cold in those days. A year in the Corps had changed his life, and he realized he had successfully stepped into the adult world.

One morning he arrived at a regular customer's home, hauled the big square of ice out of his truck with a huge set of metal tongs, and knocked on the kitchen door at the back of the house. A young woman he'd never seen before answered. She had recently moved in to take care of an elderly woman who lived there. By the time Woody set the ice in place in the bottom of the metal-lined icebox, he knew he'd found the love of his life. From that day on he looked forward to delivering ice to that house. He and Virginia got married the next year.[119]

Like Woody, most of the young men who worked in the Civilian Conservation Corps came out of the Corps ready to be adults. As Houston Pritchett in Michigan said, the Corps "was teaching us to work, we were learning something,"[120] and he and thousands of others were proud of that work and what it did for them when they left the CCC—exactly what Franklin Roosevelt pictured when he talked about saving human and natural resources.

Roosevelt had hoped that his favorite program would be made permanent—a regular government program instead of a temporary emergency measure. That didn't happen. In September 1939, Adolph Hitler's Nazi army invaded Poland, prompting Great Britain and France to declare war. A second world war had begun. The United States stayed out of direct involvement in the war until December 1941, when Japan attacked the United States at Pearl Harbor in Hawaii. Then, every resource America had—human, natural, industrial—went to defeating the Axis powers of Germany, Italy, and Japan. The need for emergency work programs evaporated—everyone was needed in the effort to win the war. As a result, the last CCC camps closed in the summer

Fire and the Forests

During the early twentieth century, the United States set aside millions of acres of land as national forests. After devastating fires threatened those forests and the towns in them, US Forest Service officials decided on a policy of suppressing—or putting out—every wildfire as quickly as possible. They believed that was the best way to protect the forests as well human life and property. The policy remained in place for several decades.

By the middle of the century, new research and understanding of forest ecology led to changes in forest management policies. Scientists had found that fire is a necessary part of forest life. Fires clear the forest floor of dead trees and brush that would otherwise fuel much larger and more destructive fires. The ash left by fires renews the soil and the forest's strongest trees are left with the fertile soil, sunlight and water they need to flourish. It seemed leaving most fires to burn was the best course.

Today, however, the warming climate means more months of fire danger and bigger, more destructive fires. At the same time, many more people live near the edge of wildlands and forests. Foresters must balance the needs of the forests with protecting human life and property. Federal agencies now work with tribal, state, and local governments to educate communities on the value of forest fires and on ways to manage those fires and protect themselves from danger. People of the twenty-first century are learning to live *with* fire as many of their ancestors did.

of 1942. But the good work the Corps had done in developing human resources became more important than ever.

Hundreds of thousands of former CCC enrollees enlisted in the military when the war started. In fact, nearly 90 percent of CCC recruits, close to three million CCC alumni, served in the military during World War II, and the military was very glad to have them.

Remember that millions of boys growing up in the 1930s had rough childhoods. They didn't go to school regularly or have rules to follow. Often, their parents had no choice but to tell them to leave home when they turned sixteen or seventeen so the younger children would have more to eat. Many young men were angry or constantly hungry and frightened. Men like that had a hard time making the transition to the discipline and physical demands of the military. Civilian Conservation Corps alumni came to military service with several advantages.

Most men who'd been in the CCC were physically fit. The months or years of good food and hard work had paid off. And the military reserve officers who ran the CCC camps had taught their men how to follow orders and take pride in their work. Recruits had also learned to interact with men very different from themselves and understood the value of teamwork. And they had experience with outdoor life and living in close quarters, the way military personnel would.

James Wilkins, who worked for the Forest Service and became a camp superintendent in the George Washington National Forest, later joined the US Army Air Forces. He discovered that he relied on men who'd been in the CCC. "They'd had some training, they had discipline, plus they had been trained to operate bulldozers, jackhammers, to use dynamite; they'd been taught to do things and they knew what to do." He believed that young men from the Corps were more likely to have success in their lives than men without that experience.[121]

Houston Pritchett went back to Detroit when he left the CCC, but during the war, he joined the army. As he described it, "coming up through the CCC gave you that know how, to get in there and get it done. The CCC made me a man, made me respect discipline."[122] The military needed all the young men like that it could get.

Though the Corps had never taught any military skills, many CCC men had more to offer the military than strong backs and good discipline. The CCC had given them civilian skills the armed forces needed.

Arthur Emory, for example, learned to fix trucks while he was at Big Meadows. As a result, when Arthur joined the navy, he became a machinist helper and worked fixing engines on military vehicles.[123] CCC drivers became military drivers. CCC company clerks became military company clerks. Some, like Bill Cameron from Ohio, worked as radio operators for their military camps because they had taken radio classes and joined camp radio clubs in the CCC. When Bill joined the army in 1940, he was sent to a post that trained men in military communications. "Because of my previous experience in the CCC as a radio operator, I was assigned as an instructor," he said.[124] Bill taught new radio operators the vital skills they needed to keep units in contact with their headquarters and one another during the war.

The men of the CCC used the skills they learned in the Corps outside the military too. One recruit who'd been a writer for his camp newspaper became a writer in a Hollywood movie studio. Others found jobs in business offices because they'd learned to do paperwork and typing. And of course, the tens of thousands who learned to read and write or who graduated from high school in the Corps could move into jobs that were closed to young men who hadn't had those opportunities.

Leo Ruvolis grew up in a small coal-mining community in western Pennsylvania. When he joined the CCC, he was sent to a Virginia camp and started taking classes in surveying land for road construction. Leo had never had much contact with anyone who'd gone to college, but his camp was near Lexington, Virginia, where the Virginia Military Institute and Washington and Lee University are located. He met some of the students from those schools and realized that there was a whole world he knew nothing about. He started taking more classes at camp, including courses in civil engineering, and went on to get a college degree when he left the CCC. Ruvolis became a bomber pilot during the war and was shot down and taken prisoner by German soldiers. He was lucky to survive. But after almost a year as a prisoner of war, he made it home. Leo kept going to school, kept challenging himself, and eventually became a professor at York College in Pennsylvania. It was a remarkable journey. Leo said, "I really believe the dream began in the CCC."[125]

Ruvolis went into engineering and later, computers. Others found they loved environmental work, and hundreds of former CCC enrollees spent their careers in conservation. One former recruit said he saw his "CCC experience as the main reason for my thirty-year career in the Soil Conservation Service."[126] Other men became park superintendents and forest directors. Some used the leadership skills they'd learned in the Corps.

Orville Olney of the Yakima Indian Nation in Washington State was one of seventy-five thousand Native Americans who joined the CCC. After four years with the Civilian Conservation Corps, Olney enlisted in the United States Marine Corps and served for twenty years. He could have settled anywhere he wanted to when he retired from the Marine Corps. He chose to go home to the Yakima Reservation, where he served his community as the chief of police before becoming a tribal court judge.[127]

Many who worked in the CCC wanted no more than a simple, quiet life after the turmoil of the Great Depression and World War II. Henry Rich, for example, stayed in Virginia when he left the CCC. He had a good reason—he had met a girl from Edinburg, just down Route 11 from Camp Roosevelt, at one of the local events the boys attended. He married the young lady, and they lived within a few miles of Camp Roosevelt for the rest of their lives. Rich even continued to work off and on as a hired cook at Camp Roosevelt until the Corps disbanded. The CCC had changed Henry Rich's life, and after his death some thirty years later, his daughter kept in touch with former recruits who had known him.[128]

Tyree Grydon, the track star, did the same thing. He married a local girl who he called his "angel." They stayed near her home and were married for over sixty-five years.[129] Many other young men who won the hearts of local women during their time in the Corps settled in those towns and became a permanent part of those communities too.

Like most men of the CCC, Woody Wilson served in the military during World War II. He was a ball-turret gunner, squeezing into a clear globe hanging from the belly of a B-17 bomber to operate his gun during missions. When he got home after the war was over, he discovered that people weren't using iceboxes anymore. They had switched to electric refrigerators. Woody's old job was gone, but he found work delivering feed to the same dairy farms where his father had collected milk. Then he learned how to repair the milk coolers most farmers had started using. Later, when schools and offices began installing air conditioning in the 1960s, Woody transferred his cooler repair skills to service the new systems. He worked in heating and air-conditioning maintenance for the county government until his retirement. He even worked in the schools he had attended as a child.[130]

When FDR had proposed the Corps to Congress in March

1933, he argued, "More important . . . than the material gains will be the moral and spiritual value of such work."[131] Woody Wilson, Houston Pritchett, Leo Ruvolis, and tens of thousands of other men were proof.

Enrollee John Miller, who worked in Oregon, said, "The finest achievement of the Civilian Conservation Corps is the building of the character of America's youth." Another recruit in Pennsylvania wrote as he left the Corps, "We . . . face the future with enthusiasm, feeling that we have proven ourselves men."[132] James Wilkins of the Forest Service said, "It wasn't only a case of getting a lot of work done. It was a case of saving the young population that had become drifters, getting them back into some kind of productive work and some self-respect for themselves."[133]

Comments like that would have put a big grin on Franklin Roosevelt's face.

Like the others, Woody had learned to value hard work in the Corps and continued to work hard in the years to come as he took care of his family and his community. He and Virginia cared for his mother until her death. They raised two children. Woody volunteered as a firefighter in Herndon when he wasn't at work. And he never forgot what being poor was like or what good soil can do. He grew all sorts of vegetables in his yard every summer— perhaps remembering that he'd called himself a farmer when he enrolled in the CCC—and gave bags of produce to elderly neighbors who needed help.

Sometimes on a beautiful summer day, Woody and Virginia packed a picnic and took their girls up to Skyline Drive in Shenandoah National Park. There they ate in the shade of now mature trees and looked out over the beautiful valley below. Then they drove along one of the prettiest roads in the country, and Woody showed his daughters the graceful stone walls he had helped build decades before. He was still proud of his time with the Civilian Conservation Corps.[134]

Woody certainly wasn't the only CCC veteran who showed his children what he'd done in the Corps. Thousands of other men did the same. Houston Pritchett stayed in Detroit after the war. He worked for over thirty years at the Ford Motor Company there, always a city man. But one summer Pritchett took his granddaughter to see the forest area where he'd worked all those years ago. Yes, he'd faced racism in the Civilian Conservation Corps. And yes, that racism and discrimination were a big disappointment to him. But in spite of the Corps' shortcomings, he was grateful to Franklin Roosevelt. As he described it, the Corps "taught you to have a backbone and stand up for yourself."[135] It was a lesson he never forgot.

Pritchett's granddaughter looked down at the vast forest spreading below them that day and then started telling everyone around them that her grandfather had planted all those trees. Houston Pritchett laughed at that, but he'd always been proud of the part he, a poor city boy, had played in building a wilderness. It pleased him that his granddaughter was proud of him too.[136]

. . .

The men of the Civilian Conservation Corps could see what they'd accomplished. They could show it to others. They knew they'd left quite a legacy. But there was more to that legacy than what their children and grandchildren could see from a mountain road.

The view from Skyline Drive in Shenandoah National Park.

CHAPTER 11

Lasting Legacies

The Civilian Conservation Corps remains today the biggest conservation project ever organized. But all big public and private programs cause controversy and make mistakes, and the CCC—with the double goal of conserving both human and natural resources—was no exception. Though most Americans of the 1930s praised the Corps with good reason, there was some serious criticism at the time and there still is today.

One criticism of the CCC was an economic concern. The Corps employed more than three million young men across the country. But critics complained that the government spent more on CCC workers than it did on workers in other programs. That was true. Of course, most workers hired during the Depression lived at home and received nothing more than a salary. CCC enrollees worked in the middle of nowhere and had to be fed and housed. At its height, the CCC had enrollees at over 2600 camps. Expenses for those camps added up. But even supporters of the program realized that the federal government was spending more than it was collecting in taxes during the Great Depression. That had never happened during peacetime before. To many people, those deficits could not be justified no matter how much good a

What's a Deficit?

Governments collect money from taxes, fees, and tariffs (taxes on goods coming into the country from other countries). They spend this money on roads, the military, law enforcement, disaster relief, and other services and programs the government provides. When a government spends more in a year than it takes in, it has a *deficit* or shortfall. It then borrows money, which must be paid back later. When a government takes in *more* than it spends, it has a *surplus*. A *balanced budget* means that the government spends about the same amount of money in a year as it takes in. In recent years the federal government in the United States has had large deficits year after year. That trend continues as of 2018, when the deficit was the largest in history.

program did. In their view, the CCC was beyond what the government should have been doing.

Segregation was a human resources issue. Though most Americans at the time supported segregation, some progressives like Harold Ickes and Frances Perkins, who worked for the government, as well as progressives who didn't, criticized the decision to segregate companies by race. They saw the policy as a clear violation of the law establishing the Corps. Integration might have cost FDR support in the South and other places, and no order from the president could change the attitudes of whites who objected to having African American workers near their homes. But to progressives then and most people now, nothing makes discrimination right.

Defenders of the president have noted that FDR appointed more African Americans to government positions than any president before him. And with the CCC, he assigned about forty African American reserve officers to command black camps and ordered the appointment of black educational advisers and work foremen for those camps.[137] But critics argue that that didn't make up for ignoring the spirit of the antidiscrimination amendment.

Issues of race scarred the CCC, and that scar remains. And though the Corps had no influence on segregation laws in the South, the African American men who worked in those states were hit with double discrimination. National parks didn't fully integrate until the 1950s, and state parks in the South were segregated until the 1960s. Picture the black men who worked in places like First Landing State Park in Virginia. They fought mosquitoes, snakes, and sweat to build the park. Yet when they finished, they couldn't visit the park or show their families what they'd accomplished because the park was whites-only.

Louder critics attacked the Civilian Conservation Corps for what it did with *natural* resources. Many conservationists supported the CCC at first, but later they decided that a number of Corps projects did more harm to the environment than good. Attempts to get rid of mosquito-borne diseases like malaria in swampy areas, for example, led to the destruction of millions of acres of swampland. Draining swamps helped control the spread of disease, but it destroyed the habitats of many animals and plants and upset the natural balance of the local ecosystems. We know today that wetlands are home to thousands of species of plant and animal life and that they control flooding more effectively than anything humans can do. Less was known in the 1930s, but Roosevelt understood that wetlands were important. He succeeded in making the Florida Everglades a national park and preserved the Okefenokee Swamp in Georgia. But that didn't help the wetlands that were lost.[138]

Opponents also spoke out about the Corps' forestry work and the Forest Service policy of preventing or putting out all fires. Clearing dead trees and wild vines took away the natural fertilizer that decaying or charred wood and plants provide to the fragile soil on the forest floor. It also destroyed animal habitats, especially for some kinds of birds. In fact, the removal of dead trees in the national forests was one reason that bald eagles— the nation's symbol—were almost extinct by 1940.[139] Certainly, bird-lover Franklin Roosevelt never intended to harm birds. But when humans interact with nature, there are often consequences that no one expects. And since the CCC moved very quickly on hundreds of projects, there wasn't time to study the possible consequences in advance as environmental impact studies do today.

The Corps made mistakes in other kinds of work as well. For example, recruits in North Dakota planted buckthorn trees to protect farmland from wind erosion. But what seemed like a good idea had a downside. The new trees weren't native to North Dakota, and their pollen created severe allergy problems in the region.[140] In Georgia, the CCC planted kudzu vines to hold the soil in place and provide feed for livestock. The vines worked and the recruits were told to plant as many of them as they could. Sixteen-year-old enrollee Lee Brown had grown up in the area. He worked in an African American company assigned to the hot, sweaty, hard-on-the-back work in rural Georgia. As he described it, "We were like the Johnny Appleseeds of kudzu."[141] But like the buckthorn trees in North Dakota, the vines in Georgia were an invasive species—they didn't grow in that area naturally. The kudzu quickly choked out other plants, climbed walls, fences, tree trunks, and hillsides, and is still a problem eighty years later.

Preservationists criticized CCC projects in the national parks.

They argued that roads, trails, and campgrounds in the parks stole the parks' wildness and ruined wilderness lands that should have been preserved just the way they were. All those people hiking and driving and camping in the parks could end up destroying the very places they'd come to see.

The criticisms went on—some unfair or exaggerated, but many reasonable.

All those flaws are the negatives of the CCC's legacy. Do the positives, the CCC's accomplishments, outweigh its mistakes?

In his 1938 address to Congress, President Roosevelt reminded Americans that for many years, the nation "went forward feverishly and thoughtlessly until nature rebelled, and we saw deserts encroach, floods destroy, trees disappear, and soil exhausted."[142]

The CCC was Roosevelt's attempt to address nature's rebellion. Most historians and environmentalists who have studied the Civilian Conservation Corps agree that while the program had serious flaws, it had extremely good outcomes for the men who participated, for the nation's land, and for the way Americans think about conservation.

Let's start with the parks.

The men of the Civilian Conservation Corps worked in nearly one hundred new or existing national parks. They worked on roads, trails, and campgrounds, and they also built visitor centers and cabins that fit into the natural landscape of each park.

Those structures are now treasures of American architecture.

The CCC established or improved over eight hundred state parks as well. In fact, some states got their very first parks because of the Corps. And every state saw its park system expand. Land for state parks nationwide grew by 70 percent while the CCC existed.[143] Virginia, for example, had no state parks at all in 1932. By 1942, the CCC in Virginia had built Shenandoah National Park, Skyline Drive, the Blue Ridge Parkway, and six state parks, and had restored five major historical sites.

In 2016 the National Park Service recorded over 325 million visitors—both American citizens and foreign tourists—entering national parks in the United States. That number is very close to the country's total population. Close to 800 million visitors entered state parks (there are more state parks than national parks, and many people go to nearby parks several times a year). Rich or poor, able to hike or in a wheelchair, living in the countryside or in a big city, most Americans can now enjoy and appreciate nature in the nation's parks. The CCC is largely responsible for that.

Other Civilian Conservation Corps accomplishments between 1933 and 1942 are less obvious but just as important.

In simple numbers, the men of the CCC put 3,400 fire lookout towers where there had been almost none. They built over forty-five thousand bridges and restored nearly four thousand historic structures—from places like the Chesapeake and Ohio Canal in Maryland to Native American ruins in the Southwest. They also helped preserve Civil War battlefields, including Vicksburg in

Mississippi and Gettysburg in Pennsylvania. Recruits worked in all forty-eight states, the District of Columbia, Alaska and Hawaii (both became states in 1959), Puerto Rico, and the Virgin Islands.

Bigger numbers help create a picture of the Corps' real impact. Think about these statistics:

The CCC completed:

• 13,000 miles of trails in the nation's parks—if all those trails were in one straight line, a person could walk from Los Angeles, California, to Boston, Massachusetts, over four times.

• 68,000 miles of firebreaks (strips of cleared land designed to stop the spread of forest or grass fires)—flying over them in a jet going close to six hundred miles per hour would take nearly 115 hours.

• 89,000 miles of telephone lines—enough to stretch from the North Pole to the South Pole seven times.

• 125,000 miles of roads—a road this long could circle the equator five times.

Miles measure length, the distance from here to there. Square miles and acres measure area—the size of a farm or state or country. Think in square miles and acres for a while, keeping in mind that one acre is about the size of a football field and one square mile equals 640 acres. The men of the Civilian Conservation Corps:

• built campgrounds on 52,000 acres of parkland—that's enough land for a football field at every public and private high school and college in all fifty states and the District of Columbia.

• repaired and replanted 814,000 acres of range for sheep and cattle grazing, about as much land as would fit in a square measuring thirty-six miles on each side.

• reduced or eliminated tree and plant disease and harmful pests in twenty-one million acres of forest and swamps, an area about the size of Indiana.

Those numbers may be impressive, but set them all aside for a moment and focus just on this one number. In nine years, the men of the Civilian Conservation Corps planted 3,000,000,000 trees. THREE BILLION. That's three thousand million trees.

If those trees were planted three feet apart in a straight line, the line could circle the earth sixty-eight times. It could reach to the moon seven times.

In the end, more than half of all the forest planting ever done in the history of the United States was done in the nine years of the Civilian Conservation Corps.[144]

What do all these numbers add up to?

Imagine looking out the window of an airplane on a cross-country flight. Much of the landscape below is a legacy of the Civilian Conservation Corps. The Corps restored seashores like Cape Hatteras in North Carolina and the dense forests of the Appalachians, as well as the soil of places like Tallapoosa County, Alabama. The CCC protected and preserved the golden grasses, grains, and grazing lands of the Great Plains and the pristine wilds of the Rocky Mountains. The Corps also saved the Joshua trees and cacti of the Mojave Desert and the temperate rain forest of the Olympic Peninsula on the Pacific Coast. These treasures might have been lost to erosion, fire, or development by now if not for the work of the Civilian Conservation Corps.

Altogether, the CCC rescued nearly 120 million acres of land, and the farmland the CCC helped renew saw significant increases in the production of beans, grains, cotton, and more.[145] Roosevelt was right. Good agricultural practices could repair even the devastation of the Dust Bowl.

Good practices can also prevent future disasters of that kind if farmers and ranchers are informed and careful. Today the Soil Conservation Service established by FDR is known as the Natural Resources Conservation Service and is a key agency of the Department of Agriculture. The agency's mission has not changed—it is there to provide scientific research and assistance to farmers and ranchers so they can improve and protect their land. Its work has paid off. The country experienced serious droughts in the 1950s and the 1980s, but the damage they did was nothing like the Dust Bowl. That was due to the work that had been done to conserve soil and teach farmers the best agricultural practices. In the early twenty-first century, the United States remains the largest producer of agricultural goods in the world.

Scientists who had criticized some of the Corps' work began to educate people about their concerns. That led to the start of several conservation organizations such as the Wilderness Society and the National Wildlife Federation. Today, the NWF has over four million members nationwide, most of them ordinary people who want to do something to protect wildlife, forests, clean water, wetlands, and more.

Keep in mind that some three million men—nearly five percent of the adult males in the nation in 1935—served in the Civilian Conservation Corps. That's a lot of Corps alumni going back to cities, towns, and farms with new appreciation for conservation. At home, many of those men formed conservation organizations in their states and towns. A club founded by former CCC recruits in Kentucky, for example, worked to restore wildlife habitats. Corps alumni living near the Great Lakes organized to protect shorelines and clean water.[146] And thousands of men of the CCC shared their concerns for nature and conservation with their children. By the 1950s and sixties, those young people had started a new environmental movement.

The work of the Civilian Conservation Corps pushed scientists, government agencies, and ordinary Americans to think about what conservation really means. How could the United States protect its natural resources *and* allow businesses to use them? How could Americans also make sure that ordinary people could explore and enjoy the incredible beauty of the nation's wild areas for generations to come? Experts disagreed on the answers, but they knew they couldn't ignore the questions.

After World War II, several states set up programs modeled

on the Civilian Conservation Corps. The federal government never reestablished the CCC as FDR had hoped, but more recent presidents—both Democrats and Republicans—have supported legislation to protect land, wildlife, air, and water. In 1970 President Richard Nixon signed a bill establishing the Environmental Protection Agency. Now a cabinet department, its mission is to protect human health and the environment through scientific research and education. The EPA also enforces the environmental laws passed by Congress—laws banning the use of chemicals that cause disease and pollute water and limiting the use of fuels that pollute the air. Today lumber companies that cut trees on public land must pay fees, which the Forest Service uses to plant new trees. Wild animals are protected from overhunting and from the loss of their habitats under the Endangered Species Act, also signed into law by Richard Nixon. Those laws work. The bald eagle, for example, is no longer in danger of extinction.

Men like Houston Pritchett and Woody Wilson lived to see their legacy in the landscapes around them. They also saw it in the concern new generations had for the environment. But protecting the CCC's legacy in the years to come will require serious effort.

The first president of the twenty-first century, George W. Bush, didn't make conservation a priority during most of his time in office. Conservationists strongly criticized him. But shortly before he left the presidency, Bush acted to set aside an enormous area of the Pacific Ocean near Hawaii. The goal was to save the rare species of fish and birds that live there and to preserve the delicate coral reef beneath the sea.

Barack Obama, president from 2009 to 2017, earned praise from conservation groups for pushing to update the Endangered Species Act and for restricting coal mining on public lands. He also set aside hundreds of thousands of acres of public land where Native American cultural areas and ancient fossils were in danger.

During the Obama years, however, the National Park Service budget approved by Congress didn't provide enough money for needed improvements and repairs to parks. Visitors could see the neglect. President Donald Trump, who took office in 2017, approved millions of dollars to help the parks begin to catch up on maintenance, but experts worried about his policies on environmental issues.

In 2017 and 2018, conservationists criticized President Trump in several areas. He was the first president in American history to reduce the amount of protected public land in the United States. His administration proposed significant increases in permits for oil and gas drilling by private businesses on public land as well. Trump also eased rules so that mining companies could dump more waste into local streams and rivers. And he called for serious budget cuts to environmental programs and scientific research. Like several presidents of the late 1800s and the 1920s, President Trump focused on making public land available for increased business use with as little regulation as possible. Critics argued that these policies would result in increased pollution and the destruction of natural resources. They also feared that the nation's wild public lands would be ruined for the future.

Perhaps the biggest environmental concern of the early twenty-first century is climate change, not an issue for political leaders of the 1930s. Scientists warn that recent warmer average temperatures around the world are caused in large part by human activity, just as the Dust Bowl was. Scientific evidence strongly indicates that the earth's warming is a major reason for the severe storms that have threatened coastlines in the last decade and is also a cause of the devastating wildfires that burn millions of acres of national forestland each year. Environmental and climate experts see a very serious need for stricter, not looser, regulations on industry in order to limit the pollution and loss of trees that warms the atmosphere and to protect public land and water.

Many people take the national parks, forests, and seashores of the United States for granted. National parks have been called "America's best idea," and it's easy to assume they will always be as magnificent as they are today. Americans are also used to having abundant, affordable food from our agricultural land and endless clean water. But will the next generation or the one after that still benefit from these resources? Will the United States continue to find a balance between using public lands for enjoyment and business, and protecting them from destruction? The American people own the public lands in the United States. The taxes Americans pay hire the federal government to manage those lands. Franklin Roosevelt had said in 1931, "The green slopes of our forested hills lured our first settlers and furnished them the materials of a happy life. They and their descendants were a little careless with that asset."[147]

By voting him into office, Americans of the 1930s hired Franklin Roosevelt to restore and protect the assets Americans had been careless with. Roosevelt established the CCC with that responsibility in mind. He told the earliest Corps enrollees, "The nation will owe you a debt of gratitude a hundred years hence [from now]."[148]

How can Americans today repay that debt? Perhaps the best way is to work to protect the national parks and forests, grasslands and wetlands, seashores and refuges that are the Civilian Conservation Corps' gift to us.

Bibliography

"African Americans in the Civilian Conservation Corps." New Deal Network. http://newdeal.feri.org/aaccc/, accessed 8/11/17.

Allen, Frederick Lewis. *Since Yesterday.* New York: Harper and Row, Publishers, 1939.

Alter, Jonathan. *The Defining Moment: FDR's Hundred Days and the Triumph of Hope.* New York: Simon & Schuster, 2006.

Baird, Lawrence. "A Quick Biography." CCC Legacy, February 2, 2008. www. ccclegacy.org/naccca. Not available as of 8/11/17.

Barkdoll, Chanda Helsley. "Camp Roosevelt" (academic paper, 1996), quoted in CCC Legacy, April 2005. http://www.ccclegacy.org/2005_April.html, accessed 8/10/17.

Bindas, Kenneth J., ed. *The Civilian Conservation Corps and the Construction of the Virginia Kendall Reserve, 1933–1939.* Kent, Ohio: Kent State University Press, 2013.

Breedon, Preston. Interview, September 25, 1999. Shenandoah National Park. https://www.nps.gov/shen/learn/historyculture/upload/ccc_oral_history_ preston_breeden.pdf, accessed 8/15/17.

Breitman, Jessica. "Frances Perkins: Honoring the Achievements of FDR's Secretary of Labor." FDR Presidential Library and Museum, accessed 8/14/17.

Brinkley, Douglas. *Rightful Heritage: Franklin D. Roosevelt and the Land of America.* New York: HarperCollins Publishers, 2016.

Brinkley, Douglas. *The Wilderness Warrior: Theodore Roosevelt and the Crusade for America.* New York: HarperCollins Publishers, 2009.

Bushman, Mark. "George Washington, the Farmer." Natural Resources Conservation Service, US Department of Agriculture. https://www.nrcs.usda.gov/ wps/portal/nrcs/detail/national/newsroom/features/?cid=nrcseprd1316224, accessed 8/14/17.

"Camp Roosevelt Beginnings." Civilian Conservation Corps Legacy. http:// ccclegacy.org/Camp_Roosevelt_68B9.php, accessed 8/15/17.

"CCC Oral Histories." Shenandoah National Park, Virginia, National Park Service. https://www.nps.gov/shen/learn/historyculture/cccoralhistories. htm, accessed 8/14/17.

"Celebrating Our Past, Creating Our Future: Recognizing the Contributions of the Civilian Conservation Corps (C.C.C.) to Maryland's State Forests & Parks." Maryland Department of Natural Resources. http://dnr.maryland.gov/centennial/Pages/Centennial-Notes/CCC_History_Part_I.aspx, accessed 8/15/17.

The Civilian Conservation Corps: Shaping the State Forests and Parks of Massachusetts. Massachusetts Department of Environmental Management, January 1999.

Civilian Conservation Corps Museum. Stafford Springs, CT.

Civilian Conservation Corps (CCC) Enrollee Records, Archival Holdings and Access.

http://www.archives.gov/st-louis/archival-programs/civilian-personnel-archival/ccc-holdings-access.html, accessed 8/10/17.

Cohen, Adam. *Nothing to Fear: FDR's Inner Circle and the Hundred Days That Created Modern America.* New York: Penguin Press, 2009.

Cohen, Adam. "The First Hundred Days." *Time*, June 24, 2009.

http://content.time.com/time/specials/packages/article...html, accessed 8/14/17.

Cohen, Stan. *The Tree Army: A Pictorial History of the Civilian Conservation Corps, 1933–1942.* Missoula, MT: Pictorial Histories Publishing Co., 1980.

Collier, Christopher, and James Lincoln Collier. *Progressivism, the Great Depression, and the New Deal, 1901–1941.* New York: Benchmark Books, 2001.

Dant, George. "The Early Days." Speech given at Camp Roosevelt reunion, September 1991. http://www.ccclegacy.org/Camp_Roosevelt_68B9.php, accessed 8/10/17.

Davis, Frank C. *My C.C.C. Days: Memories of the Civilian Conservation Corps.* Boone, NC: Parkway Publishers, Inc., 2006.

Davis, Ren, and Helen Davis. *Our Mark on This Land: A Guide to the Legacy of the Civilian Conservation Corps in America's Parks.* Granville, Ohio: McDonald and Woodward Publishing Co., 2011.

Downey, Kirstin. *The Woman Behind the New Deal: The Life and Legacy of Frances Perkins—Social Security, Unemployment Insurance, and the Minimum Wage.* New York: Anchor Books, 2009.

Drake, Kerry. "The Deadly Blackwater Fire," WyoHistory.org, July 2, 2016. https://www.wyohistory.org/encyclopedia/deadly-blackwater-fire, accessed 1/22/19.

Dukes, Jesse. "Making Room for Shenandoah National Park." Public Radio Exchange, May 1, 2008. https://beta.prx.org/stories/26740#description, accessed 8/12/17.

Engle, Reed L. *Everything Was Wonderful: A Pictorial History of the Civilian Conservation Corps in Shenandoah National Park.* Luray, VA: Shenandoah National Park Association, 1999.

Engle, Reed. "Shenandoah: An Abused Landscape?" Shenandoah National Park, Virginia, National Park Service. https://www.nps.gov/shen/learn/historyculture/abused_landscape.htm, accessed 8/14/17.

Engle, Reed. "Shenandoah National Park Landscape and the CCC." Shenandoah National Park, Virginia, National Park Service. https://www.nps.gov/shen/learn/historyculture/cccjobs.htm, accessed 8/14/17.

Engle, Reed. "Wilderness by Design?" Shenandoah National Park, Virginia, National Park Service. https://www.nps.gov/shen/learn/historyculture/wilderness_by_design.htm, accessed 8/14/17.

"Timeline: The Evolution of the CCC." *American Experience.* http://www.pbs.org/wgbh/americanexperience/features/civilian-conservation-corps-evolution-ccc/, accessed 8/14/17.

"Fact Sheet: Natural History, Ecology, and History of Recovery." US Fish & Wildlife Service, Midwest Region. https://www.fws.gov/midwest/eagle/recovery/biologue.html, accessed 1/22/19.

"Farm Foreclosures." Encyclopedia of the Great Depression, 2004. https://www.encyclopedia.com/economics/encyclopedias-almanacs-transcripts-and-maps/farm-foreclosures, accessed 1/22/19.

Fechner, Robert. "My Hopes for the CCC." *American Forests: The Magazine of The American Forestry Association. Washington, DC, January 1939.* http://newdeal.feri.org/forests/af139.htm, accessed 8/11/17.

"Fred B. Helsley." *Civilian Conservation Corps Legacy. April 2005.* http://www.ccclegacy.org/2005_April.html, accessed 1/22/19.

Fremon, David K. *The Great Depression in American History.* Springfield, NJ: Enslow Publishers, 1997.

"George Washington National Forest." *The Forest Service and the Civilian Conservation Corps.* https://www.nps.gov/parkhistory/online_books/ccc/ccc/chap13.htm.

Giordano, Anthony. *Improving Forests and Men: The CCC Experience in Connecticut.* Southern Connecticut State University. Proquest Dissertations Publishing, 2014. Accessed 8/17/18.

Haigh, Susan. "Making Men of Boys During Depression." *The Hartford Courant*, August 18, 2008. https://www.newspapers.com/image/244104296/, accessed 8/11/17.

Helms, Douglas. "Hugh Hammond Bennett and the Creation of the Soil Conservation Service." https://www.nrcs.usda.gov/wps/portal/nrcs/detail/national/about/history/?cid=nrcs143_021383, accessed 8/21/18.

Helms, Douglas. "The Civilian Conservation Corps: Demonstrating the Value of Soil Conservation." *Journal of Soil and Water Conservation 40*, March–April 1985: 184–188. Reprinted in *NCR History Articles,* U.S. Department of Agriculture. https://www.nrcs.usda.gov/wps/portal/nrcs/detail/national/about/history/?&cid=nrcs143_021393, accessed 8/11/17.

"Henry Agard Wallace, 33rd Vice President (1941–1945)." *United States Senate.* Senate Historical Office. http://www.senate.gov/artandhistory/history/common/generic/VP_Henry_Wallace.htm, accessed 8/11/17.

Hill, Edwin G. *In the Shadow of the Mountain: The Spirit of the CCC*. Pullman, WA: Washington State University Press, 1990.

"Historical Population." Population.us. http://population.us/oh/toledo/, accessed 8/14/17.

"History of the Interior." US Department of the Interior. http://interior.gov/whoweare/history.cfm, accessed 8/14/17.

"The Hoover Story, Gallery 7: From Hero to Scapegoat." Herbert Hoover Presidential Library and Museum. https://hoover.archives.gov/exhibits/Hooverstory/gallery07/index.html, accessed 8/14/17.

Houck, Davis. *FDR and Fear Itself: The First Inaugural Address*. College Station: Texas A&M University Press, 2002.

Huggard, C. J., and Arthur Gomez, eds. *Forests Under Fire: A Century of Ecosystem Mismanagement in the Southwest*. Tucson: University of Arizona Press, 2001.

"Hugh Hammond Bennett: Father of Soil Conservation." Natural Resources Conservation Service. Reprinted from *American National Biography*, Volume 2. New York: Oxford University Press, 1999, pp. 582–583. https://www.nrcs.usda.gov/wps/portal/nrcs/detail/national/about/history/?cid=stelprdb1044395, accessed 7/5/17.

Ickes, Harold. *The Secret Diary of Harold Ickes: The First Thousand Days*. New York: Simon & Schuster, 1953.

"The inaugural parade along Pennsylvania Avenue during the 1933 inaugural ceremony of President Roosevelt in Washington DC." Critical Past. http://

www.criticalpast.com/video/65675055030_Franklin-Roosevelt_inaugural-parade_army-units-march_military-band_American-flag, accessed 8/14/17.

Justin, James. "Thirty Dollars a Day, One Day a Month!" *Biography of James F. Justin*, updated 2004. http://www.justinmuseum.com/famjustin/Justin1.html, accessed 8/11/17.

Kennedy, David M. *Freedom from Fear: The American People in Depression and War*. New York: Oxford University Press, 1999.

Kernan, Michael. "Back to the Land." *The Washington Post*, April 6, 1983. https://www.washingtonpost.com/archive/lifestyle/1983/04/06/back-to-the-land/c9f521ad-0a2f-4b37-b0d1-ff1966cc4ecb/?utm_term=.09879dbf9242, accessed 5/1/19

Kuhn, Frank, Jr. "He Traded a Jackhammer for a Paint Brush and Stylus," CCC Legacy, February 8, 2008. Not available as of 8/11/17.

Kyvig, David, E. *Daily Life in the United States, 1920–1940*. Chicago: Ivan R. Dee, 2004.

Lacy, Leslie. *The Soil Soldiers: The Civilian Conservation Corps in the Great Depression*. Radnor, PA: Chilton Book Company, 1976.

Lambert, Darwin. *The Undying Past of Shenandoah National Park*. Lanham, MD: Roberts Rinehart, Inc., 1989, 2001.

Lash, Joseph P. *Eleanor and Franklin*. New York: Signet Press, 1971.

Leuchtenburg, William E. *The FDR Years: On Roosevelt and His Legacy*. New York: Columbia University Press, 1995.

"The Living New Deal." University of California at Berkeley. https://livingnewdeal.org, accessed 8/14/17.

"Local Focus: Hugh Bennett and the Perfect Storm." *What's On Now*. WETA. https://weta.org/tv/program/dust-bowl/perfectstorm, accessed 1/22/19.

Maher, Neil M. *Nature's New Deal: The Civilian Conservation Corps and the Roots of the American Environmental Movement*. New York: Oxford University Press, 2008.

"March 4, 1933." https://www.nps.gov/hofr/upload/the%20morning%20of%20march%204.pdf, accessed 8/14/17.

McDuffie, Ann. "75th Anniversary of New Deal's CCC." Fredericksburg.com, May 24, 2008. http://www.fredericksburg.com/town_and_countycover_sto/10/17ry/th-anniversary-of-new-deal-s-ccc/article_55584b4d-af63-5437-a496-84f7db778bac.html, accessed 8/11/17.

McKibben, Bill. "A New Deal for the Environment." *The Hartford Courant*, 2008 (specific date and page number not available).

Monroe, Rob. *The CCC Boys.* Harrisonburg, VA: Virginia Public Television, 1999. DVD.

Moore, Robert. *The Civilian Conservation Corps in Arizona's Rim Country: Working in the Woods.* Reno: University of Nevada Press, 2006.

"More Than 80 Years Helping People Help the Land: A Brief History of NRCS." Natural Resources Conservation Service, US Department of Agriculture. https://www.nrcs.usda.gov/wps/portal/nrcs/detail/national/about/history/?cid=nrcs143_021392, accessed 8/14/17.

Morgan, Ted. *FDR: A Biography.* New York: Simon & Schuster, 1985.

O'Connell, Mary Louise. Interview, 10/12/14.

Paige, John C. *The Civilian Conservation Corps and the National Park Service: An Administrative History.* National Park Service Department of the Interior, 1985.

https://www.nps.gov/parkhistory/online_books/ccc/ccc5.htm accessed 8/10/17.

"Philosophy of Rugged Individualism." Miller Center, UVA. https://millercenter.org/the-presidency/educational-resources/philosophy-of-rugged-individualism.

Powell, Jim. *FDR's Folly: How Roosevelt and His New Deal Prolonged the Great Depression.* New York: Crown Forum, 2003.

"President Roosevelt Visits CCC at Shenandoah." Universal Studios, August 14, 1933, in *Encyclopedia Virginia.* Virginia Foundation for the Humanities. http://encyclopediavirginia.org/media_player?mets_filename=evm00000745mets.xml, accessed 8/15/17.

Records of the Civilian Conservation Corps. *Guide to Federal Records.* National Archives. https://www.archives.gov/research/guide-fed-records/groups/035.html, accessed 8/11/17.

Ripplemeyer, Kay. *The Civilian Conservation Corps in Southern Illinois, 1933–42.* Carbondale, IL: Southern Illinois University Press, 2015.

Roberts, Phillip M. "Boll Weevil." *New Georgia Encyclopedia.* http://www.georgiaencyclopedia.org/articles/business-economy/boll-weevil.

Roosevelt, Eleanor. Quotation from Franklin Delano Roosevelt Memorial, Washington, DC.

Roosevelt, Franklin. "Address at Oglethorpe University." *Work of Franklin D. Roosevelt,* May 22, 1932. http://newdeal.feri.org/speeches/1932d.htm, accessed 8/14/17.

Roosevelt, Franklin. "First Inaugural Address." March 4, 1933. https://www.archives.gov/education/lessons/fdr-inaugural. accessed 2/26/19.

Roosevelt, Franklin. "On Moving Forward to Greater Freedom and Greater

Security." September 30, 1934. Franklin Delano Roosevelt Library and Museum. http://docs.fdrlibrary.marist.edu/firesi90.html, accessed 8/16/17.

Roosevelt, Franklin. "State of the Union Address." January 3, 1938. http://www.thisnation.com/library/sotu/1938fdr.html, accessed 8/11/17.

Roosevelt, Franklin. "Three Essentials for Unemployment Relief." Speech to Congress, March 21, 1933. *Public Papers of the Presidents of the United States*. https://books.google.com/books?id=eibeAwAAQBAJ&pg=PA81&lpg=PA81&dq, accessed 8/16/17.

Roosevelt, Franklin. "What We Have Been Doing and What We Are Planning to Do." Radio address, May 7, 1933. http://www.presidency.ucsb.edu/ws/?pid=14636, accessed 8/14/17.

Rosenberg, Doris Wilson. Interview, 7/8/2014.

Salmond, John A. *The Civilian Conservation Corps, 1933–1942: A New Deal Case Study*. Durham, NC: Duke University Press, 1967. https://www.nps.gov/parkhistory/online_books/ccc/salmond/contents.htm, accessed 8/12/17.

Scott, Edward, and Russell Barlow. Interview. February 2, 1978. http://www.nps.gov/shen/historyculture/upload/ccc_oral_history_edward_scott_and_russell_barlow.pdf, accessed 8/16/17.

Shlaes, Amity. *The Forgotten Man: A History of the Great Depression*. New York: Harper Perennial, 2007.

Speakman, Joseph M. "Into the Woods: The First Year of the Civilian Conservation Corps." *Prologue Magazine*. National Archives, Fall 2006. https://www.archives.gov/publications/prologue/2006/fall/ccc.html, accessed 8/15/17.

Stangl, Bill. Interview, September 27, 1998. Shenandoah National Park. https://www.nps.gov/shen/learn/historyculture/upload/ccc_oral_history_bill_stangl.pdf, accessed 8/16/17.

Stone, Robert. "The Civilian Conservation Corps." *American Experience*. Aired November 2, 2009. www.pbs.org/wgbh/americanexperience/films/ccc/, accessed 8/14/17.

Tobin, James. Interview by Dave Davies, *Fresh Air*, NPR, November 24, 2013. https://www.npr.org/2013/11/25/247155522/roosevelts-polio-wasn-t-a-secret-he-used-it-to-his-advantage.

Wallace, Henry A. "Selected Works of Henry A. Wallace." New Deal Network. http://newdeal.feri.org/wallace/docs.htm, accessed 8/14/17.

Walter, Colleen Esther. *Conserving Memory: The CCC in Western Maryland*. University of Maryland–Baltimore County. Proquest, 2011, 78. Accessed 8/17/18.

Washington, George. "First Annual Address to Congress." Miller Center, UVA. https://millercenter.org/the-presidency/presidential-speeches/january-8-1790-first-annual-message-congress, accessed 1/22/19.

Watkins, T. H. *The Great Depression: America in the 1930s.* New York: Little, Brown and Company, 1993.

Watkins, T. H. *The Life and Times of Harold L. Ickes, 1874-1952.* New York: Henry Holt and Company, 1990.

Welky, David. *The Thousand-Year Flood: The Ohio-Mississippi Disaster of 1937.* Chicago: University of Chicago Press, 2011. https://books.google.com/books?id=RAGAtlHTWogC&pg=PA75&lpg=PA75&dq=civilian+conservation+corps+indiana+floods+1937&source=bl&ots=1qlmwJ-PjO&sig=p1FTDnoLSpZMyW2NPdQd8eggCU4&hl=en&sa=X-&ved=0ahUKEwjB-KDtmdzVAhUJ0IMKHedpBFYQ6AEIaDAN#v=onepage&q=civilian%20conservation%20corps%20indiana%20floods%201937&f=false, accessed 8/16/17.

White, Cody. "The CCC Indian Division." Prologue Magazine, Summer, 2016. https://www.archives.gov/publications/prologue/2016/summer/ccc-id.html accessed 2/27/19.

Williams, Gerald W. "CCC Accomplishments." *Camp Roosevelt.* www.angelfire.com/journal2/cccnews, accessed 8/11/17.

Williams, Gerald W., and Aaron Shapiro. "Looking Back: The Civilian Conservation Corps and the National Forests." *FS Today*, April 3, 2008. https://www.fs.usda.gov/Internet/FSE_DOCUMENTS/fsbdev3_004791.pdf, accessed 8/14/17.

Endnotes

1 Rosenberg.

2 Adam Cohen, "The First Hundred Days."

3 A. Cohen, *Nothing to Fear: FDR's Inner Circle and the Hundred Days That Created Modern America*, 2.

4 "Philosophy of Rugged Individualism."

5 "The Hoover Story."

6 Stone, "The Civilian Conservation Corps." *American Experience*.

7 Alter, 2.

8 "Historical Population."

9 A. Cohen, *Nothing to Fear*, 42.

10 Ibid., 16.

11 Brinkley, *Rightful Heritage: Franklin D. Roosevelt and the Land of America*, 227.

12 Mary Louise O'Connell.

13 Ibid.

14 "Farm Foreclosures."

15 James Tobin.

16 Eleanor Roosevelt.

17 Alter, 215.

18 F. Roosevelt, "First Inaugural Address."

19 Ibid.

20 Ibid.

21 A. Cohen, *Nothing to Fear*, 42.

22 Houck, *FDR and Fear Itself: The First Inaugural Address*.

23 "The Inaugural Parade."

24 Lash, 153.

25 F. Roosevelt, "Address at OU."

26 F. Roosevelt, "What We Have Been Doing."

27 F. Roosevelt, "On Moving Forward."

28 Bushman, "George Washington, the Farmer."

29 George Washington, First Annual Address to Congress.

31 Ibid., 17–20.

32 Brinkley, *Rightful Heritage*, 19.

33 Ibid., 8.

34 Ibid., 6

35 Ibid., 40.

36 "Local Focus."

37 Stone.

38 Kernan.

39 Gerald Williams and Aaron Shapiro, "Looking Back."

40 Downey, 150.

41 Engle, *Everything Was Wonderful*, 22.

42 Downey 150.

43 Engle, *Everything Was Wonderful*, 24.

44 Downey, 150–151.

45 A. Cohen, *Nothing to Fear*, 215–216.

46 Salmond.

47 "Celebrating Our Past, Creating Our Future."

48 Lambert, *The Undying Past of Shenandoah National Park*, 213–220.

49 George Dant.

50 "Camp Roosevelt Beginnings."

51 Dant.

52 Rosenberg.

53 Engle, *Everything Was Wonderful*, 23.

54 Rosenberg.

55 Ibid.

56 Downey, 155.

57 Lambert, 224.

58 Breedon.

59 Engle, *Everything Was Wonderful*, 67.

60 Ibid., 65.

61 Ibid., 86.

62 Monroe.

63 Kuhn.

64 "Camp Roosevelt Beginnings."

65 "Fred B. Helsley."

66 Barkdoll.

67 Scott and Barlow, CCC Oral Histories.

68 Ickes, 78.

69 Alter, 295

70 Colleen Ester Walter.

71 Maher, 79.

72 Ickes, 78–79.

73 "President Roosevelt Visits CCC at Shenandoah."

74 Maher, 93.

75 Stangl.

76 Speakman.

77 Maher, 79.

78 White.

79 Brinkley, *Rightful Heritage*, 416.

80 Downey, 141.

81 Salmond, Chapter 5.

82 Monroe.

83 Watkins, 641–642.

84 Ripplemeyer, 99.

85 "The Evolution of the CCC."

86 *African Americans in the CCC*.

87 Salmond.

88 Engle, *Everything Was Wonderful*, 43.

89 Breedon.

90 F. Davis, 55.

91 Ibid., 27.

92 Ibid.

93 Bindas, 86.

94 Ibid.

95 Moore, 79.

96 Ibid., 86.

97 R. Davis and H. Davis, 236.

98 "Hugh Hammond Bennett."

99 Helms, "Hugh Hammond Bennett and the Creation of the Soil Conservation Service."

100 "More Than 80 Years Helping People Help the Land."

101 Welky, 75.

102 Hill, 139.

103 Giordano, 37.

104 Lacy, 147.

105 Hill, 33.

106 Moore, 92.

107 Ibid., 56.

108 Hill, 82.

109 Ibid.

110 Drake.

111 Speakman, 110.

112 Ripplemeyer,106.

113 Ibid., 47–48.

114 Speakman, 111.

115 Ibid., 113.

116 Rosenberg.

117 Ibid.

118 Ibid.

119 Ibid.

120 Stone.

121 "George Washington National Forest."

122 Ibid.

123 Monroe.

124 Hill, 161.

125 Speakman, 195.

126 Maher, 216.

127 Hill, 129–130.

128 Camp Roosevelt Beginnings.

129 Breedon.

130 Rosenberg.

131 Franklin Roosevelt. March 21, 1933.

132 Lacy, *The Soil Soldiers*, 135, 138.

133 "George Washington National Forest."

134 Rosenberg.

135 Stone.

136 Ibid.

137 Brinkley, *Rightful Heritage*, 259.

138 Ibid., 443.

139 Fact Sheet.

140 Ibid., 475.

141 Ibid., 444.

142 F. Roosevelt, January 3, 1938.

143 Brinkley, *Rightful Heritage*, 178.

144 W. E. Leuchtenburg, in Salmond.

145 Maher, 66.

146 Maher, 218.

147 Speakman, https://www.archives.gov/publications/prologue/2006/fall/ccc.html.

148 Ren Davis and Helen Davis, 352.

149 F. Roosevelt. "Acceptance Speech."

150 "Health Insurance Coverage of the Total Population."

151 "How Obamacare Helped Slash Personal Bankruptcy by 50%."

152 Campbell.

153 "She-She-She Camps."

154 Lambert, 184–187.

155 Lambert, 255.

156 Clemens.

Time Line

1929

March

Herbert Hoover is inaugurated as the thirty-first president of the United States

October

Weaknesses in the US economy lead to a stock market crash and the beginning of the Great Depression

1932

August

Unemployment in the US reaches 25 percent

November

Franklin Delano Roosevelt is elected president of the US in a landslide

1933

March 4

Franklin Roosevelt takes the oath of office as the thirty-second president of the United States, saying people can be put to work on natural resources projects

March 9

FDR introduces to his cabinet heads a plan for hiring 500,000 young men to work on conservation projects

March 21

FDR proposes a CCC bill to Congress

March 31

Roosevelt signs the Federal Unemployment Relief Act (CCC) into law, including a provision barring discrimination

April 7

Henry Rich becomes the first enrollee in the Civilian Conservation Corps

April 17

The first enrollees in the CCC arrive at Camp Roosevelt near Luray, Virginia

April-August

The CCC opens enrollment to American Indians, World War I veterans, local experienced men (LEMs) and begins education programs open to all recruits

May 1

Walker Woodrow Wilson (Woody) enrolls in the CCC in Alexandria, Virginia

August 12

President Roosevelt visits Shenandoah National Park camps to see their work and gain further support for the program

December

Woody Wilson enrolls for a second six-months in the CCC

1934

June 30

Woody Wilson leaves the CCC after his father's death

1935

CCC enrollment reaches its peak of 500,000 men

July

Edwin Hill begins work in the CCC at Hard Labor Creek, Georgia Director Robert Fechner orders segregation for CCC camps nationwide; some camps will remain integrated despite the order

1936

November

Franklin Roosevelt is elected to a second term

1937

January

CCC workers in Utah aid sheep ranchers in severe snow and frigid temperatures

January-February

CCC workers in Ohio and Indiana participate in flood rescue and relief efforts

August

CCC workers and others killed in the Blackwater Fire in Wyoming

1938

October

Seven CCC workers killed in the Pepper Hill Fire in Pennsylvania

1939

Houston Pritchett joins the CCC in Michigan

August

Edwin Hill and other CCC workers battle extreme fires in Washington State

September

World War II begins in Europe

1940

November

Franklin Roosevelt is elected to an unprecedented third term

1941

December 7-8

The Empire of Japan attacks the US at Pearl Harbor in Hawaii; the US Congress declares war

1942

July

Congress appropriates funding to shut down remaining CCC camps

Index

A READING GROUP GUIDE TO

FIGHTING
for the
FOREST

by P. O'Connell Pearson

Discussion Questions

Chapter 1: Waiting for Hope

1. Analyze the significance/meaning of chapter one's title.

2. Why did President Herbert Hoover believe he had done all he could to help the country? What is your source for this answer? Use both the author's and Hoover's words.

3. What adjectives would you use to describe conditions in the US as Franklin Roosevelt became president?

Chapter 2: Taking Action

4. In what ways was Franklin Roosevelt well prepared to be president?

5. What led to FDR's paralysis? How did the paralysis affect his political ambitions?

6. Read the full FDR quotation in chapter two that begins with, "No country, however rich, can afford the waste of its human resources." Is this a primary or secondary source? How do you think it applies to his support for the CCC?

Chapter 3: Looking Back

7. Create a time line of American attitudes toward natural resources or a time line of key presidents in US history and their land policies.

8. Describe the environmental issues the US faced during the 1930s.

Chapter 4: A Miracle of Cooperation

9. Analyze the meaning of chapter four's title.

10. What characteristics did members of FDR's cabinet share?

11. Summarize Oscar De Priest's amendment to the Emergency Conservation Employment Act and why its passage was unusual and significant. What is your source?

12. Why did FDR think it was important to build national parks in the eastern United States?

Chapter 5: Into the Woods

13. Why were women not allowed to join the CCC?

14. Describe a typical CCC recruit.

15. Describe a typical CCC camp. Use pictures from the book as well as text to gain information.

Chapter 6: What Will They Do, Mr. President?

16. What happened to the people who lived on the land that became Shenandoah National Park? How did those people respond?

17. Why didn't the CCC use advanced technology and machines to make the work faster?

18. List some of the most common types of work the men of the CCC did in building Shenandoah National Park.

Chapter 7: Winning Support

19. Why was FDR concerned about public support for the CCC? Use a primary source from the chapter to support your answer.

20. How did CCC camps help nearby towns economically? Give examples.

21. Describe the experience of African American and Hispanic recruits in the CCC.

Chapter 8: More Than Work

22. List some of the opportunities offered to CCC recruits when they were not working. Which do you think had the greatest impact on the young men?

Chapter 9: Across the Country

23. Describe two kinds of CCC projects outside the parks.

24. What adjectives would you use to describe Ed Hill's experience in the CCC?

25. How did the CCC improve its safety record over time?

Chapter 10: Moving On

26. Why did many adult men suffer from depression during the economic crisis?

27. How did experience in the CCC prepare young men for military service during WWII?

28. Find two or three quotations from former CCC enrollees. Describe their feelings about their experience.

Chapter 11: Lasting Legacies

29. Make two columns. In one column, list negative outcomes of the CCC's organization and projects. In the other column, list positive outcomes. Discuss with a partner.

Extension Activities

1. Primary and Secondary Sources

Look through the sources listed in the book's bibliography and identify ten primary sources and ten secondary sources. Be sure you can explain why you identified each source as you did.

2. Vocabulary

As you read, make a chart of words or terms that were new to you or that you were unsure of, particularly words or terms related to government, history, or economics. Define each word or term and choose ten words to use in sentences.

3. CCC Geography

On a map of your home state, mark the locations where the CCC worked. Conduct research to find out if any CCC camps or structures still exist in your state.

On a map of the United States, mark the parks, forests, or historic sites you have visited. Conduct research to find out if the CCC worked in any of those places.

4. Time Line

Create a time line of significant conservation and environmental projects and legislation in the US since 1933.

5. You Are the Reporter

Imagine you are a reporter in 2003, the seventieth anniversary of the CCC. You plan to attend a reunion of CCC men who are now in their late eighties and nineties. Make a list of questions you would like to ask them.

6. You Are the Recruit

Find the location of a CCC camp near your home and the

kind of work the men did there. Imagine that you are a member of a unit at that camp, and write a letter home describing your experience to your family. Be sure to use information from pictures as well as text.

This guide was created by the author of Fighting for the Forest, *P. O'Connell Pearson. She is a former history teacher with a master's degree in education from George Mason University. She has contributed to and edited history textbooks and published articles in magazines and newspapers including the* Washington Post. *Always enthusiastic about sharing the stories of history, she earned her MFA in writing for young people from Lesley University and now writes both historical fiction and nonfiction.*

Looking for another great book?
Find it
IN THE MIDDLE.

Fun, fantastic books for kids
in the in-be**TWEEN** age.

IntheMiddleBooks.com

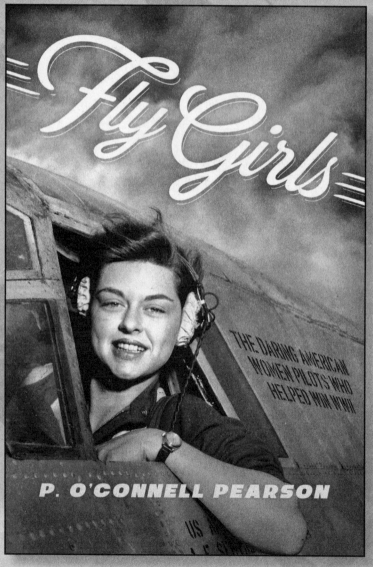

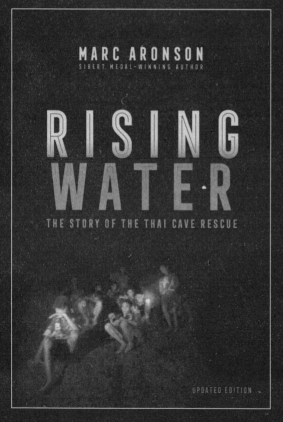